How to be a

MORE EFFICIENT

RADIOLOGIST

A Guide to Practice, Reporting, and

Workflow Optimization

Online Resources

Efficiency-Oriented Macro Library:
https://tinyurl.com/fast-rad-macros

Peripheral Device Links:
https://tinyurl.com/fast-rad-gear

AutoHotKey Scripts:
https://tinyurl.com/fast-rad-ahk

How to be a

MORE EFFICIENT RADIOLOGIST

A Guide to Practice, Reporting, and

Workflow Optimization

LONG H. TU, MD, PHD

Department of Radiology and Biomedical Imaging
Yale School of Medicine,
New Haven, CT, USA

First Edition, Salem Publishers, November 2023.

ISBN: 9798218324025

Disclaimer

Every effort has been made in preparing this book to provide accurate information in accordance to policies and practice at the time of publication. Nevertheless, the authors, editors, and publishers can make no warranties that the information contained herein is totally free from error, not least because clinical standards are constantly changing through research and regulation.

The authors, editors, and publishers therefore disclaim all liability for direct or consequential damages resulting from the use of material contained in this book.

For my family.

Preface

One of the most valuable skills a radiologist can develop is how to efficiently review and report studies. In residency and fellowship, much of the explicit training focuses on the identification and characterization of abnormality. Professional testing and certification also primarily address the ability to *accurately* diagnose. In independent practice, however, one of the greatest predictors of professional satisfaction and overall productivity is work efficiency – a skill not often formally taught.

The absence of formal efficiency-oriented curricula may be because trainees do generally become faster with time and greater experience. Resultant disparities in work efficiency are often thought to be inherent or otherwise considered non-modifiable. However, deeper investigation of what accounts for variation in work speed suggests that almost all radiologists could take steps to optimize their work processes. It is also useful to recognize that while there are often wide variations in speed, faster radiologists are not necessarily less accurate. In some cases, the opposite may be true.

It is crucial to distinguish "reading fast" and "working efficiently." Trainees and attending radiologists, when seeking to improve their speed, may attempt to merely perform work tasks at a faster pace. Granted, we all have an ability to temporarily heighten the attentiveness and effort applied to a task before us. However, at a certain point, merely working faster becomes unsustainable. In the worst scenario, radiologists may seek to improve their speed by cutting corners or examining studies in a less careful fashion. These are obviously not advisable, and furthermore, not effective strategies in the long term.

The objective of this book is instead to improve work "efficiency." This involves a large suite of techniques that a radiologist may use to improve the speed with which they complete their work, without sacrificing quality. These include though are not limited to optimizations in study approach, PACS workflow, dictation tools, IT infrastructure, and work environment. Small differences in efficiency across the variety of domains that compose radiologic practice add up to produce large variations in the ability of individuals to perform clinical work. These differences subsequently impact professional satisfaction, the productivity of group practices, the timeliness of patient care, and the capacity of radiologists to make contributions beyond clinical throughput.

In the remainder of this book, we will refer informally to being a "faster" radiologist or to the "speed" of work. In all cases, what we have in mind are the improvements that arise from greater *efficiency*. In contrast to the pitfalls of naïve "speed reading," we will discuss strategies that produce greater productivity per unit effort or even which improve "speed" and accuracy *simultaneously*.

This book is inspired by our shared experiences working with trainees and colleagues and observing how differences in efficiency impact not just the professional lives, but also indirectly, the wellbeing and personal lives of radiologists. With the advent of remote and hybrid work, trainees must contend with increasingly fragmented apprenticeship. In-person teaching has always had to compete with the demands of clinical work. This book is aimed at both passing on some of the practical wisdom that is increasingly hard to come by as well as freeing up more time for quality mentorship, teaching, and other activities.

Obviously, not all variation in efficiency can be accounted for or modified using the techniques in this book. However, the strategies we discuss can help trainees and radiologists hone their abilities to the greatest extent possible. I hope this book provides a useful guide on your journey in becoming the best – most accurate, thoughtful, efficient, and happy – radiologist you can be.

Long H. Tu, 2023

Make it better

Do it faster

Makes us stronger

– Daft Punk (2001)

Table of Contents

Acknowledgements

This work would not have been possible without the help, input, and insight of numerous co-authors and collaborators. They are listed at the beginning of each chapter and together on the following page. In particular, I would like to highlight the incredibly talented trainees who provided contributions with utmost professionalism, responsiveness, and attention to detail. Peter Hung, Nadia Solomon, Cyrus Safinia, Spencer Beck, Kevin Wu, Kyle Tegtmeyer, Lam (Bi) Tu, and Alexander (Alex) Kuehne – thank you so much for your thoughtful suggestions and writing. Many thanks to my medical student research assistant, Quoc-Huy Ly, for your help on this and numerous other projects. This work would not be nearly as good without all of your help.

I would like to thank Dr. Jamal Bokhari, our residency program director, for his encouragement in disseminating this work. I owe a debt of gratitude to Drs. Jason Teitelbaum and Amit Mahajan for their assistance in crafting a mix of clinical commitments that has allowed my continued writing and engaging with trainee education. I would also like to acknowledge the broader guidance of Drs. Richard (Rick) Bronen, Howard (Howie) Forman, and Rob Goodman, who have helped me navigate recent academic life. Many other mentors, advisors, and collaborators, too numerous to mention here, have helped me find my footing as faculty. Thank you all.

I would also like to credit the members of our PI³ (Program for Innovation in Imaging Informatics) group, particularly Drs. Melissa Davis and Joseph (Joe) Cavallo, whose enthusiasm for programmatic improvement has inspired several topics in this book. I am incredibly grateful to Jitendra (Jeetu) Bhawnani and Heather Hogle for their support of IT-based optimizations at our own program. Many thanks to my good friends Drs. Brooke Schrickel and Mehmet Adin for their commentary and feedback on many aspects of this work, beyond where it is more formally indicated.

Everything I have, I ultimately owe to the unwavering support of my parents. I would also like to credit Salem and Lily (my dogs) for bringing consistent joy and humor to my life. And finally, thank you Gresi, for all the ways you've been there for me these past few years.

Contributors

S. A. Jamal Bokhari, MD
Professor of Radiology
Yale School of Medicine

Mahan Mathur, MD
Associate Professor of Radiology
Yale School of Medicine

Spencer Beck, MD
Radiology Resident
Yale-New Haven Hospital

Jason Teitelbaum, MD, MBA
Assistant Professor of Radiology
Yale School of Medicine

Alexander Kuehne, MD
Radiology Resident
Yale-New Haven Hospital

Nadia Solomon, MD MS
Radiology Resident
Yale-New Haven Hospital

Margarita Revzin, MD
Associate Professor of Radiology
Yale School of Medicine

Cicero Silva, MD
Professor of Radiology
Yale School of Medicine

Cyrus Safinia, MD
Radiology Resident
Yale-New Haven Hospital

Lam Tu, DO
Radiology Resident
Rutgers New Jersey Medical School

Quoc-Huy Ly, BS
Medical Student
SUNY Downstate College of Medicine

Mehmet E. Adin, MD
Assistant Professor of Radiology
Yale School of Medicine

Rahul Hegde, MD
Assistant Professor of Radiology
Yale School of Medicine

Melissa Davis, MD, MBA
Associate Professor of Radiology
Yale School of Medicine

E. Brooke Schrickel, MD
Assistant Professor of Radiology
Ohio State College of Medicine

Kyle Tegtmeyer, MD
Radiology Resident
Yale-New Haven Hospital

Peter Hung, MD
Neuroradiology Fellow
Yale School of Medicine

Christopher Gange, MD
Assistant Professor of Radiology
Yale School of Medicine

Kevin Wu, MD
Radiology Resident
Yale-New Haven Hospital

Joseph Cavallo, MD, MBA
Assistant Professor of Radiology
Yale School of Medicine

Why Developing Efficiency is a Training Priority

Long H. Tu

Spencer Beck

Syed A. Jamal Bokhari

Introduction

Work efficiency influences a variety of domains including patient care, interservice relationships, radiologist work satisfaction, and the broader evolution of medical practice. Understanding this influence can help motivate efforts at developing efficient practices, tools, and infrastructure.

Patient care

Work efficiency can have a positive indirect impact on the quality and safety of patient care. Interpretive errors in radiology have been found to increase with greater shift length and study volume. Errors are more common after 8-10 hours of continuous work and at the end of shifts, likely related to visual fatigue, mental fatigue, and a sense of urgency to finish work. Reducing the total time and effort spent on any given study can decrease the overall effort required for radiologists to complete a specified work volume. Improved efficiency (holding work volume constant) can allow radiologists to take breaks, consult colleagues, and avoid excessive time at the workstation – all factors which can improve diagnostic accuracy.

In all medical practice, there is a tension between depth of evaluation and the speed of work completion. Ideally, the time and effort spent on each case varies according to study complexity and length. Greater overall efficiency can allow for increased flexibility to dedicate sufficient time to complex cases. In acute settings such as in stroke care (where "time is brain"), timeliness of reporting directly impacts patient outcomes. In urgent settings, timely reporting prevents calls to the reading room about already delayed reports which can lead to a vicious cycle of interruptions and further delays. In almost all cases, timely reporting improves the anxiety and uncertainty experienced by patients, patient families, and clinical colleagues.

More broadly, we must recognize that radiology results are often the rate-limiting step of patient disposition in acute, urgent-care, and hospital settings. Recent national hospital bed shortages and crises in emergency department boarding emphasize how efficient care at all levels can improve patient experiences.

Radiologist work satisfaction

Radiologists within a practice may differ in speed by a factor of greater than 200%. While it is not clear that most radiologists would be able to double their speed with specific additional training or workflow changes, more modest improvements on the order of 10% are achievable by early-stage attendings. Essentially all trainees could make even larger gains in efficiency.

Using approximate figures, we can estimate the time and monetary value of improved efficiency for the average radiologist. The typical radiologist's career spans 30 years. Radiologists work about 50 hours/week for 44 weeks a year. In 2023, the average U.S. radiologist annual salary is around $500K/year. We can estimate that a usual career in radiology spans approximately 66,000 hours, with lifetime earnings of approximately $15 million in 2023 U.S. dollars.

Over the course of such a career, a mere 1% improvement in efficiency would save 660 hours of work. This amount of time is equivalent to 13 weeks of vacation or $150K in (pre-tax) work-equivalent earnings. A 10% improvement in efficiency is equivalent to more than two years of (continuous) vacation time and more than a million dollars of life-time earnings. On the high end, radiologists increasing their work efficiency by 100% (a factor of two) would recapture more than a decade's worth of work time and tens of millions of dollars of equivalent effort. Even if our point estimates are overly optimistic by a factor of 2x or 3x, the amount of personal time and value at stake remains large and meaningful.

Consistent development of efficiency-oriented skills in training and practice is likely to produce improvement between the middle and high estimates (10-100%). Earlier investment into practice efficiency may also produce compounding benefits through freeing more time for other areas of practice development and physician wellbeing. Although difficult to quantify, the peace of mind arising from a greater ability to "manage the list," and the downstream impacts on "work-life balance" are equally if not more valuable.

Broader medical practice

No matter the nature of one's career, no radiologist practices in a completely independent manner. The speed of one radiologist can have both direct and indirect impacts on others in their group. Work satisfaction in group practices often depends on a feeling that everyone is contributing fairly. Work efficiency impacts the reputation of individual radiologists, group practices, and even larger medical systems. The ability of individuals to navigate the job market, or for groups to win hospital contracts, is in part influenced by the ability of radiologists to provide timely care.

Investing in efficacy is not just the domain of community and private practice radiologists. Improved work speed also has benefits in academics and is valuable for any radiologist with non-clinical responsibilities. Teaching, administration, quality improvement, and research all require substantial time and attention. For those whose careers require juggling commitments, optimizing efficiency is a pathway to "doing it all" without sacrificing work-life balance.

Conclusion

There seems to be a gap in the formal instruction incorporated into residency and fellowship training. New graduates without dedicated training may not have the skills to thrive in environments with ever-increasing volume. Even if a hundred of hours of education early in training were required to develop a 1% improvement in speed, our estimates suggest that this would produce a greater than 500% return on investment over the course of a career. Therefore, developing efficiency must be a priority for all trainees and early-career attending radiologists. This book can provide an overview of key techniques to prevent burnout and perhaps even thrive in the modern radiology workplace.

Selected references

- Lee CS, Nagy PG, Weaver SJ, Newman-Toker DE. Cognitive and system factors contributing to diagnostic errors in radiology. American Journal of Roentgenology. 2013 Sep;201(3):611-7.

- Alexander R, Waite S, Bruno MA, Krupinski EA, Berlin L, Macknik S, Martinez-Conde S. Mandating limits on workload, duty, and speed in radiology. Radiology. 2022 Aug;304(2):274-82.

- Janke AT, Melnick ER, Venkatesh AK. Hospital occupancy and emergency department boarding during the COVID-19 pandemic. JAMA Network Open. 2022 Sep 1;5(9):e2233964-.

- Your Income vs Your Peers': Medscape Radiologist Compensation Report 2023. https://www.medscape.com/slideshow/2023-compensation-radiologist-6016378?icd=login_success_email_match_norm#1. Accessed: 11/15/2023.

How to Use This Text and a Few Caveats

Long H. Tu

Spencer Beck

Syed A. Jamal Bokhari

Introduction

For trainees in the earliest part of residency and on non-acute services, it is important to note that building a foundation of knowledge and reporting according to attending preferences may be a higher priority than efficiency. It is useful to strike a balance in the development of practical as well as fundamental knowledge. Only once a foundation is built does efficiency provide further value.

The first half of this book is especially relevant to trainees preparing for emergency or independent call. Topics including study approach, PACS use, and efficient dictation offer the greatest benefit to trainees though are relevant to radiologists at any career stage.

Topics discussed in the later chapters are more applicable to radiologists that have greater control over their practice setting. Optimizing clinical workflow, work environment, and hardware are approaches that are of the highest yield for those preparing for the transition to attendinghood as well as those already practicing independently. The sections on optimizing macros and automation tools are likely to provide useful strategies for all readers.

Consider the audience

For trainees, the supervising attending is the first audience of the radiology report. However, reports will ultimately serve a wide range of people. Referring clinicians, other radiologists, patients, patient families, business staff, and in some cases legal personnel may all ultimately rely on report contents. In subspecialty practice, referring services may have specific preferences when it comes to the structure or details of radiology reports. In our role as consultants, it can be helpful to learn these preferences and tailor our reports to these primary audiences. As we discuss various strategies to improve reporting efficiency, it is important to consider whether any given approach is appropriate for the clinical and professional context.

Background knowledge

In this text, we will focus on practical efficiency-oriented topics. There is however, no replacement for the extensive conventional training in residency and fellowship required to develop an intuitive understanding of pathology on medical imaging. Workflow optimization by itself cannot guarantee quality care. In many cases, confidence in one's own medical knowledge and abilities is synergistic with practical skills in improving efficiency.

Scope of material

This text focuses on strategies most relevant to general and emergency radiology. As a result, where modality-specific, we are mostly concerned with common radiographic, CT, and ultrasound exams. We will touch only briefly on less common MRI exams. Wherever possible, we will indicate principles which are universal to practice in radiology.

Relative importance of domains

Modifications to one's workflow will have differing relative impact on overall efficiency depending on the processes which are improved or automated. To provide a sense of how important each domain is to overall workflow optimization, we estimate the following relative impact on maximal work efficiency:

- Dictation Optimization (~40%)
- Study Approach and PACS Optimization (~30%)
- Physiologic and Mental Optimization (~10%)
- Hardware Optimization (~10%)
- Other Workflow Optimizations (~10%)

Conflicts of interest

In this text we will refer to specific dictation, PACS, and electronic medical record software. Similarly, we will mention example hardware accessories which can be used to improve work efficiency. The authors of this text have no professional or business relationship with any vendors and derive no financial benefit from their mention. The inclusion of specific software and hardware tools is intended only to maximize the utility of information presented and is not meant as an endorsement of any particular product. In many cases, experience with specific devices or software may be incidental to practice setting.

Final caveats

It is important to emphasize that the strategies we discuss here are tools, rather than universal recommendations. The perspectives on PACS use, dictation, and workflow management are not applicable to all scenarios or practice settings. There is no one right way to provide efficient and high-quality care in radiology. However, it can be useful to consider a variety of techniques and apply them where appropriate or draw inspiration to develop one's own approaches. Each reader is responsible for assessing the appropriateness of any given method for their own practice setting. Furthermore, readers will benefit differently from workflow improvements. Many factors that impact work efficiency are not as easy to modify, such as IT infrastructure, extent of prior training, and some variation in inherent work speed.

Lastly, this text represents a synthesis of wisdom from practicing radiologists with the recommendations from the best available literature. While we aim to be comprehensive, not all technologies or approaches are necessarily included. This book is also produced by a small team of writers, editors, and designers; it will be inevitably imperfect in expression and representation of diverse practice scenarios. Please consider validating any approaches against local expertise.

Ultimate objectives

The aim of this work is to help future radiologists save thousands of hours or millions of dollars-worth of effort for the sake of both patient care and personal wellbeing. It is critical to recognize however, that we function within a larger healthcare system with often vested and sometimes perverse incentives. The viability of radiology as a specialty depends not just on providing services as efficiently and accurately as possible, but also on providing greater value and more impactful guidance. Many challenges face our field: the advent of machine learning based technologies, increasing imaging volume and complexity, and a medical system often driven by profit rather than true benefit to patients. We would encourage readers in a position to positively impact the field to consider how reclaimed time can be used in service of higher aims.

Overarching Principles in Improving Efficiency

Long H. Tu

Alexander Kuehne

Margarita Revzin

The big picture: more high-level work

Most improvements in efficiency arise from maximizing the proportion of time that a radiologist spends doing what only they can do: evaluating and interpreting images, consulting on complex cases, and advising on further evaluation.

Routine or ancillary tasks such as loading/preparing images, accessing the medical chart, enumerating findings, and proof-reading should be done as easily (with as minimal effort) or in as automated a fashion as possible. Other tasks that do not require a radiologist's expertise, such answering phones, scheduling, and contacting other staff would ideally be handled by support staff. In this text, we will examine means by which the demand of these peripherals can be lessened, so that more attention can be devoted to radiologist-specific tasks.

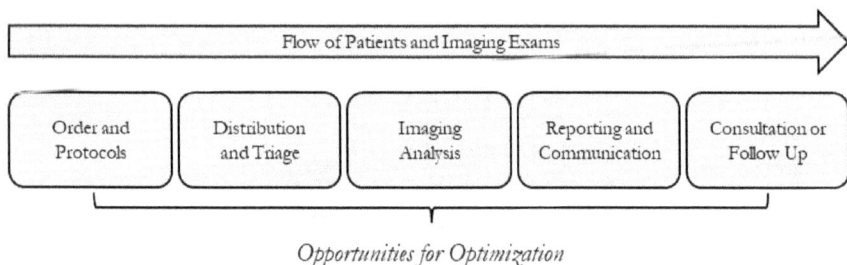

Flow of Patients and Imaging Exams

| Order and Protocols | Distribution and Triage | Imaging Analysis | Reporting and Communication | Consultation or Follow Up |

Opportunities for Optimization

Figure: Domains of radiologic workflow amenable to efficiency-oriented improvement.

Minimize redundant work by developing checklists

Radiologists early in their training are rightfully preoccupied with detecting as many relevant findings as possible. The steep learning curve and frequent errors made in the first years of residency can produce a sense of distrust in one's own abilities and insecurities in one's fund of knowledge. The understandable anxiety that arises from this experience can compel trainees to review the same study again and again, hoping to detect abnormalities that were not seen in their first evaluation. Over time, greater knowledge and experience allows trainees to move on from studies with confidence that they applied due diligence. Not all trainees develop this confidence equally, and for some, persistent worry can hamper efforts to develop reasonable efficiency.

Several approaches can help trainees develop confidence in the thoroughness of their evaluation. Chief among these is the conscious development of detailed checklists ("search patterns") for each study type or clinical scenario. This topic has been covered more thoroughly in articles, teaching videos, and books which are both easily accessible and, in many cases, publicly available. As such, we will touch only on the relevance of such processes in the development of practice efficiency.

Know which findings are "critical" to detect

A large part of the education in residency is obtained through "read outs" with supervising radiologists or through reviewing edited reports. At each stage of training, it is valuable to recognize which corrections are related to stylistic preferences and which correspond to true errors in interpretation or detection, which may impact patient care. Attending radiologists should help trainees recognize these differences. Trainees should be encouraged to ask questions when they are unsure, and furthermore, to invest early on in obtaining the necessary clinical and radiologic knowledge that will help them make the distinction themselves.

From a practical perspective, it is useful to accumulate a list of "do not miss" findings for any given study. Trainees and radiologists with greater experience can also develop a personalized list of their own blind spots. Attending radiologists may benefit from recognizing the blind spots of their trainees. It can additionally be useful to mentally enumerate the common and easily missed entities for any clinical indication. Having personalized internal checklists (which one can doublecheck after the application of broader search patterns), can provide reassurance that one has applied thorough evaluation to each study.

As a simple example, for chest radiograph, critical and potentially life-threatening findings include:

- Misplaced lines or malpositioned endotracheal tube
- Ectopic air (e.g., pneumothorax, pneumomediastinum, and pneumoperitoneum)
- Lung nodule (possible cancer)

For CT head examination, critical and serious abnormalities include:

- Acute intracranial hemorrhage
- Acute ischemic stroke
- Mass lesion/mass effect
- Hydrocephalus

Once one has addressed the clinical question, carefully inspected the whole of the anatomy, and doublechecked for pertinent negatives and positives, one can more confidently and efficiently move to the next case. While it would be ideal for radiologists to detect and describe all abnormalities in every case, we are not immune to human error. Therefore, if there is one category of findings to which we should dedicate extra care, it is those with the greatest potential impact on patient outcomes.

Although comprehensive lists of potentially critical findings are beyond the scope of this text, it is helpful to recognize that the most serious and life-threatening conditions commonly fall into a small number of categories. The "big three" are acute vascular pathology, aggressive infectious/inflammatory processes, and neoplastic/metastatic disease. In specific clinical scenarios, high-risk pathologies may also include misplaced devices, obstructive processes, and trauma.

Understand the epidemiology of error

A brief review of the different types of errors that radiologists make may assist in developing the "meta-cognition" required for confidence in practice. Of all errors made in radiologic practice, error in detection by far is the most common type, constituting 60-80% of cases. Detection error is also the largest contributor to malpractice suits against radiologists, a reasonable proxy for the subset of errors which produce serious adverse outcomes. In one representative study, the most common error leading to litigation was missed breast neoplasm. The next most common errors leading to lawsuits were missed non-spinal and spinal fractures, other malignancies (most commonly lung and gastrointestinal cancers), and vascular lesions. Issues with communicating findings and recommending follow-up studies were relatively uncommon (comprising less than 5% of all litigated errors).

What we can learn from these trends is that, as you evaluate studies, if you have looked carefully for the most common neoplasms (breast, prostate, lung, and bowel), fractures, and vascular lesions, you will have avoided the vast majority of preventable serious harm (and subsequent possible litigation) due to misdiagnosis. Along with consistent adherence to one's search pattern, this knowledge can help reduce the anxiety that produces redundant review of studies in a fashion that may not improve diagnostic yield.

As trainees become more experienced, the number of missed or misinterpreted abnormalities decreases. While all radiologists should strive to become as accurate as possible, it is realistic to expect that we will all continue to make errors. Studies estimate detection errors to occur in 3-5% of all interpretations done by attending radiologists in routine practice. What matters the most is that if errors occur, they have as little clinical impact as possible.

Conspicuously absent from studies of adverse outcomes and/or legal action involving radiologists are harms from insufficient hedging or awkward report wording. While clear and appropriately hedged reports are valuable for other reasons, this should provide further reassurance that stylistic preferences generally do not impact care. So long as the important abnormalities are detected and appropriate recommendations are made, other efforts are of secondary importance.

Learn to see patients and studies as a "whole"

As one becomes more experienced, it becomes easier to hold the entirety of a patient's presentation and study findings in working memory. This task-specific enhanced cognition, which is well-documented in other professions, allows a radiologist to see each patient as a whole and quickly identify the most important findings amongst the "noise".

Focused chart review is often as important as imaging analysis in providing effective care. Indications provided for imaging requisitions are often incorrect, incomplete, or otherwise misleading. Understanding the fuller clinical context is associated with improved diagnostic accuracy, clinical relevance of reports, and reporting confidence. Focused attention to anatomy and pathology of concern can both expedite and improve the sensitivity of visual analysis.

A more holistic view also allows radiologists to understand each finding within the context of unifying pathologic processes, rather than relying on real-time dictation as a memory aid. Critical as well as incidental findings are ultimately attached to a "feeling" or intuition as to how they will impact the downstream care of the patient.

This overarching and holistic view of patients helps guide more efficient reporting and clinically impactful consultation and recommendations. Less time can be spent on observations deemed unlikely to influence care. While this skill can arise naturally, it can also be consciously developed earlier in training.

Trainees may consider scanning whole examinations prior to dictation and attempting to form an initial "impression." This initial review can then be checked against conclusions which arise from a conventional approach, in which all findings are enumerated and then accounted for in subsequent analysis. With practice, the accuracy of visual inspection without dictation can approach or surpass that in which dictation is used as a memory aid. In particular, complex cases can cause inexperienced radiologists to "lose the forest for the trees." The goal of previewing the whole case prior to beginning dictation is to see the "forest" first. With enough practice, this approach is enough to guide reporting entirely from memory.

Recognize the "buckets" of clinically impactful findings

An extension of knowing which findings are the most critical to detect is recognizing that radiologic exams can be organized into "buckets" by the change in management that occurs because of the findings. The most important task of a radiologist is to make sure that each patient makes it into the correct "bucket" – receives the appropriate change in care. Slight variations in reporting style, description of abnormality, and even minor errors which do not alter patient management are *much* less important than those variations which alter the "bucket" (category of management) to which the patient is directed.

For example, in the setting of trauma, the detection or miss of a single non-displaced rib fracture is unlikely to alter patient care. Pain management and supportive measures will be provided whether or not a fracture is present. However, missing a fracture that motivates the diagnosis of flail segment – for example, one of five fractures at adjacent ribs or one of three segmental fractures at adjacent ribs – can negatively impact care. This is because flail segments may be managed differently: with positive pressure ventilation or surgical fixation. Patient care and, therefore, outcomes are impacted if the patient is not appropriately categorized.

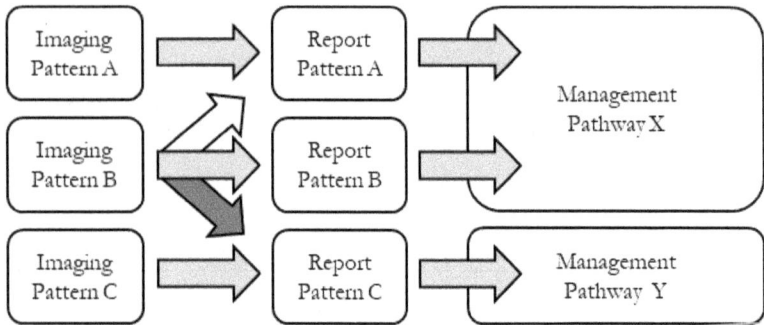

Figure: Conceptual diagram reflecting the sorting of cases into appropriate "buckets." Variations in reporting or even small errors that do not alter management (e.g., describing imaging pattern B via report pattern A) are not as consequential as those that can change management (e.g., describing imaging pattern B via report pattern C).

If the correct change in management is produced, a radiologist may be reassured they have facilitated the best possible outcome. The radiologist can also be reassured against legal risk as any variation in reporting or practice must be a *proximate cause* of patient harm to motivate medicolegal events. Variations which do not impact management (generally) cannot harm patients. Obviously, even minor errors are best avoided, and reporting of abnormality can aid in explaining symptoms or provide reassurance even when there is no change in management. However, the concept of sorting patients based on management can increase radiologist awareness that not all errors or variations in care are equal.

Whether a finding is clinically impactful or not depends on the clinical context. For example, the significance of any lung nodule depends on its morphology, the presence of other nodules, patient age, and cancer history, among other factors. Clearly, the level of detail that a radiologist must apply in analysis and description is guided by a broader understanding of "what matters" in medicine. This is the reason why during training and practice, it is crucial to continually build one's understanding of how radiologic findings impact downstream management.

The interaction of radiology with other aspects of medicine is only partially addressed by conventional educational materials and training. Attention to the broader medical literature, following one's own "interesting" cases, and engaging clinical colleagues in discussion can help maintain this knowledge base. Cultivating a sense of curiosity for how we impact patient outcomes can also contribute to a sense of meaning and purpose, in addition to providing an avenue for greater efficiency.

Examples of findings or descriptions which may not impact care (and might be omitted):

- Asymptomatic anatomic variations, aside from treatment planning studies or other very specific scenarios. (We learn about these in training, and should be able to recognize them, though it is not strictly required to describe them in all scenarios.)
- The specific dimension of new lung nodules in a patient who has already has pulmonary metastases sufficient in extent that no change in care is likely.
- The details of stable degenerative spine disease on CT/MRI studies in a patient who is terminally ill and is unlikely to receive specific intervention for chronic spinal degeneration.
- Soft tissue laceration or edema on extremity radiographs, that should be clinically apparent and will not alter management.
- Soft tissue laceration or edema on CT head/spine studies, that are known or should be clinically apparent and will not alter management. (Exceptions: soft tissue gas concerning for infection, radiopaque foreign bodies, or displacement of fat planes that could suggest joint effusion, possible as a result of occult trauma or infection.)

Where relevant, consider tailored search patterns

Early in training, trainees develop search patterns which help cover the relevant anatomy for each exam type. This is a good strategy to avoid missing important abnormalities. However, as a radiologist becomes more experienced, they may begin tailoring their imaging analysis approach to specific exam indications or protocols. In addition to a search pattern for each body part and modality, the radiologist has in their "toolkit" refined approaches for numerous specific scenarios. These alternative approaches can provide further improvements in efficiency.

One modification that can be helpful, is to *first* look for suspected abnormalities, *then* evaluate the remaining anatomy in systematic fashion for incidental and unexpected findings. Alternatively, some radiologists will look at "everything else" prior to the area of interest, then focus on the known or suspected abnormality. Either of these are reasonable and viable strategies. Such tailored search patterns are not necessarily faster in all cases, but can be helpful when suspected abnormality is concentrated in a single anatomic region or set of images.

These alternative approaches can improve efficiency by allowing the radiologist to offload the mental effort required to evaluate complex *known* pathology, before beginning the usual search pattern. Often the search through remaining anatomy can be performed more quickly, since there are fewer additional findings. Any additional findings are often straightforward to report. Separating the search pattern into two phases can reduce errors related to satisfaction of search. If expected abnormities are encountered in the middle of a usual search pattern and a large amount of time or mental effort is required to characterize the abnormality, it is easier to forget to look at the remaining anatomy afterward. This is a scenario where small gains in efficiency can be synergistic with improved accuracy.

For example, a radiologist might carefully examine the surgical site on a CT for abdominal pain after bowel resection, then scan the remaining anatomy for incidental and unexpected abnormality. A radiologist might first compare multiple sclerosis plaques on FLAIR and post-contrast sequences of a brain MRI, prior to a systematic evaluation of other anatomy and images. In the acute setting, it can be useful to quickly try to answer the clinical question (e.g., is there acute appendicitis?) prior to the usual systematic approach.

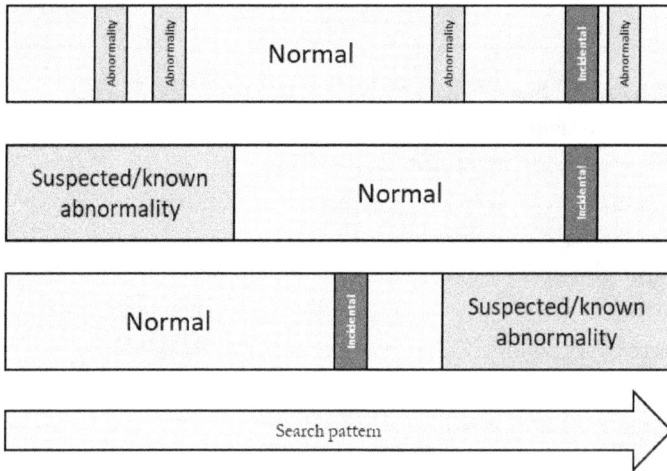

Figure: Schematic diagram of conventional search patterns (top bar) vs. tailored search patterns (middle and bottom bar) where suspected or known abnormality is evaluated all together, either at the beginning or end of visual inspection. Evaluation of the remaining anatomy can be performed more quickly in search of incidental or unexpected abnormalities.

Other examples of scenarios where it may be useful to split the approach into distinct phases:

- Follow up of oncologic/staging studies where there is complex involvement of structures, e.g., head and neck cancers.
- Follow up of complex fluid collections or abscesses after a previous episode of ruptured appendicitis, diverticulitis, or other perforated viscous.
- Assessing for changes in post-repair aortic aneurysms or dissections.
- Assessing for new hemorrhage on head CT after thrombolysis of stroke.
- Assessing for new spinal fractures in a patient with extensive existing osseous metastatic disease or prior numerous fractures.
- Assessing for osseous/soft tissue injuries on a trauma patient.

Selected references

- Whang JS, Baker SR, Patel R, Luk L, Castro III A. The causes of medical malpractice suits against radiologists in the United States. Radiology. 2013 Feb;266(2):548-54.
- Bruno MA, Walker EA, Abujudeh HH. Understanding and confronting our mistakes: the epidemiology of error in radiology and strategies for error reduction. Radiographics. 2015 Oct;35(6):1668-76.
- Waite S, Scott J, Gale B, Fuchs T, Kolla S, Reede D. Interpretive error in radiology. American Journal of Roentgenology. 2017 Apr;208(4):739-49.
- Castillo C, Steffens T, Sim L, Caffery L. The effect of clinical information on radiology reporting: a systematic review. Journal of Medical Radiation Sciences. 2021 Mar;68(1):60-74.
- Tu LH. Search Pattern: A Systematic Approach to Diagnostic Imaging. Independently Published; 2020 Jun 30.

PACS Interface Optimization

Long H. Tu

Alexander Kuehne

Margarita Revzin

Introduction

Visual inspection of imaging exams in PACS is the centerpiece of modern radiologic practice. While there are limits to how quickly a radiologist can view images, many processes in image evaluation can be improved to maximize practice efficiency. Streamlining study loading, improving conspicuity of abnormality on images, and developing better means of navigating studies can all improve work efficiency. Computer aided detection, including AI applications, can help identify findings such as intracranial hemorrhage and lung nodules faster and with more confidence.

Invest early in learning hotkeys for all commonly used PACS functions

Perhaps the most important early investment that both trainees and radiologists can make is to become familiar with all PACS shortcuts as soon as possible. Each of the most commonly used tools in PACS should be accessed with a single keystroke or mouse button. Use of a tool palette requiring right click, selection from a menu, or clicking on button in the PACS interface are far too slow for functions that may be performed hundreds of times in a shift. One should not have to search on the screen to access any commonly used tool.

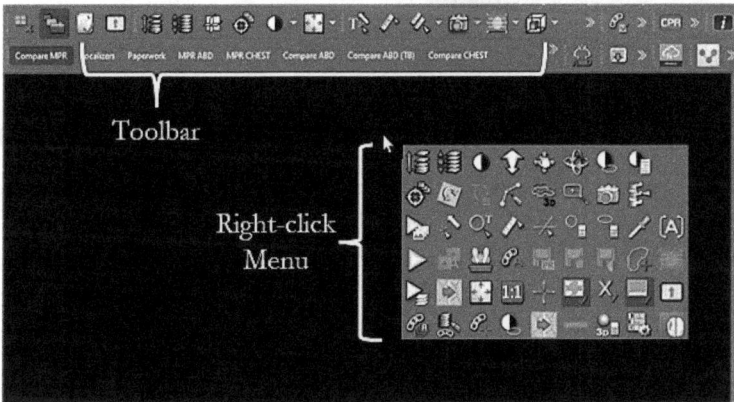

Figure: Right-click menus and interface tool bars are inefficient, requiring visual search, mouse movement, and additional clicks to access tools. We recommend against their use for common tools.

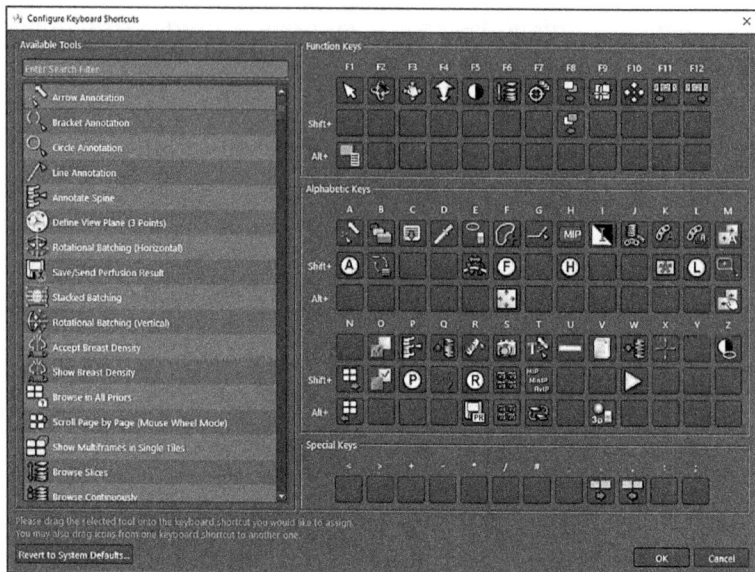

Figure: Assigning tools to keyboard hotkeys that can be accessed with a single action is faster and preferrable. In our PACS (Visage), global hotkey assignment can be performed from a menu accessed with the shortcut "Ctrl +K."

An essential means of becoming familiar with one's PACS interface is to find the global hotkey reassignment or reference tool. The following functions are examples of those which should be made immediately accessible and ideally a part of "muscle memory":

- General: Windowing, auto-window, leveling, scrolling/zoom, panning.

- Special functions: invert, spine numbering, import comparison dates (if available.)

- MPR view: 3D localizer/triangulation, toggle MIPs/MinIP/AvIP, change slice thickness, reset axis, link scroll, 3-D overlay studies, co-register 3-D overlaid studies.

- Analysis: ruler, angle measure, region of interest, arrow.

- Other: save/copy image (send to clipboard), automatically scroll image stack/study, next annotated image, next hanging protocol.

We strongly recommend investing in learning the keyboard shortcuts to the above functions, or those most relevant to one's practice, as soon as possible. The investment of a few minutes will return many hours of work life.

By extension, it is useful, every time one begins working with a new PACS (e.g., for fellowship or a new job) to dedicate time within the first 1-2 weeks to become as familiar as possible with the new hotkeys. This is also the time to reassign hotkeys to the keyboard, programmable mice, or other peripheral devices. Planning to do this as soon as possible provides the greatest dividends for one's investment and is worth dedicating time even beyond usual work hours. Earlier familiarization can prevent the development of inefficient habits (accessing tools through multiple clicks) that develop without proper preparation.

Leverage multiplanar reconstructions (MPR) for faster viewing of cross-sectional imaging

Many workflows for CT/MRI evaluation include the routine production of thick-slice reformatted images. However, in some PACS, a dynamic MPR viewer can provide more efficient means of assessing images than default image stacks.

Using these systems, radiologists may reconstruct thin-section (raw) images into axial, coronal, and sagittal views on the fly. PACS may also allow real time control of obliquity and slice thickness. Hotkeys can be used to toggle between AvIP, MinIP, and MIP views (average, minimum, and maximum intensity projections respectively). Navigating image data using these functions can markedly reduce the time that is necessary to detect and characterize pathology.

Differing anatomy and pathology require differing reconstructions, slice thickness, and "intensity" projections. A good rule of thumb is to use a viewing perspective that lays out the anatomy of interest in as few image slices as possible. Obliqued views may be useful to assess ribs, vessels, ureters, and other structures that do not conform to standard slice orientations. Relatively "bright" abnormalities are best detected with MIPs. "Dark" abnormalities are best seen with MinIPs. Anatomy or pathology with differing intensity or with complex morphology is best evaluated with AvIP projection. Dynamically toggling between differing slice thicknesses, windows, and projections can maximize one's ability to understand findings quickly.

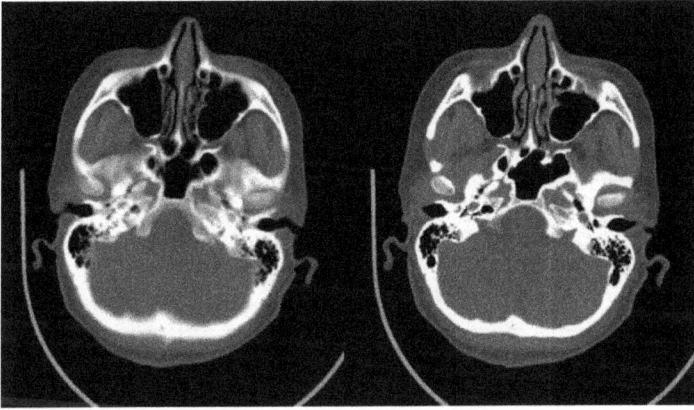

Figure: Thick-slice axial AvIPs (left panel) can be helpful to assess the symmetry and integrity of the skull base foramina. Notice how both foramina ovale and zygomatic arches are visible on a single image, allowing faster screening for abnormality. Subtle anatomic detail could be investigated with thinner slice images (right panel) as warranted.

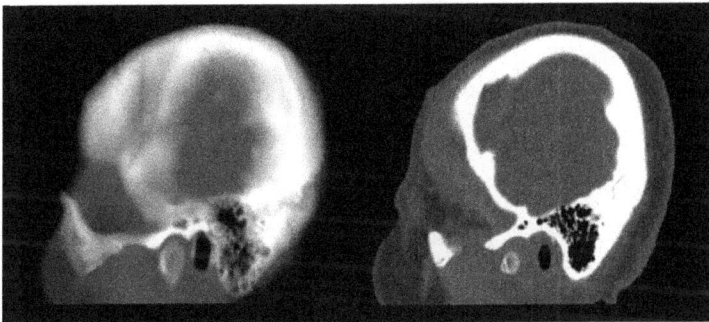

Figure: Thick-slice AvIPs in differing projections (left panel) can be helpful to assess other osseous structures based on shape and orientation. Notice enhanced anatomic visibility and thus improved evaluation of the zygomatic arch and temporal calvarium on a single image compared to thin-slice reconstructions (right panel).

Suggested projection(s) for screening evaluation	Anatomy or pathology
Axial/coronal/sagittal MIPS	Brain enhancing lesions
Axial MinIPs	Intracranial susceptibility (SWI)
Coronal/sagittal MIPs	Neck arteries
Axial/coronal MIPs	Lung nodules
Axial/coronal AvIPs	Renal exophytic lesions
Coronal/sagittal AvIPs	Bowel
Coronal/sagittal AvIPs and MIPs	Mesenteric arteries
Oblique axial/coronal/sagittal AvIPs	Rib fractures and lesions
Coronal/sagittal AvIPs	Osseous pelvis

Table: Suggested projections for reviewing select anatomical sites and pathology. Additional views may be useful for further characterization of findings.

Consider overlapping rather than book-ended image stacks

In some cases, smooth scrolling of overlapping medium-thickness slices (e.g., 2-4 mm) can provide an optimal balance between spatial resolution and contrast resolution. Most conventional image stacks are constructed in a book-ended fashion, which are visually perceived as "jumps" from one image to another without shared underlying data between slices. In contrast, with overlapping slices, any abnormality will be present on a greater number of images – reducing the risk of detection error. Medium thickness reconstructions also allow greater contrast resolution (better signal to noise ratio) than thin slices and higher spatial resolution than thick slices. Greater conspicuity allows for faster scrolling while maintaining high sensitivity for abnormalities. Finding the best trade-off in spatial and contrast resolution for each part of one's search pattern can produce a meaningful improvement in overall efficiency.

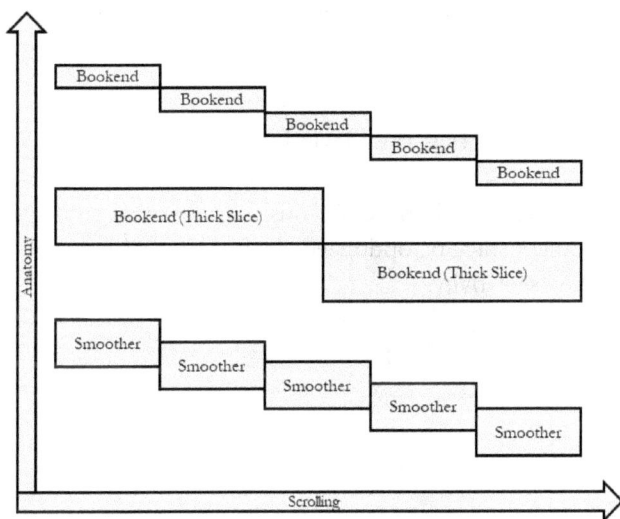

Figure: Schematic diagram of bookended thin (top) and thick slices (middle) vs. smoother scrolling medium or thick slices (bottom). Smoother scrolling slices share imaging data between adjacent images and can provide a balance between spatial and contrast resolution.

Optimize windowing and leveling for different anatomic sites and imaging acquisitions

Most radiologists learn early in training to switch among different window and level presets for lung, soft tissue, and bone. However, each CT acquisition and each sequence in an MRI exam differs based on numerous patient-level and technical factors. Preset windows and levels should be considered only a first approximation to optimal viewing parameters for any given image stack. Furthermore, each anatomic sub-site or suspected pathology may require finer-grain adjustments to optimize window and level.

For example, manual narrow windowing to look for subtle liver lesions is better than using preset soft tissue windows. The ideal window will depend on many technical and patient-level factors. Patient size, artifact, contrast bolus timing, and other factors impact lesion conspicuity and ideal windows. On brain MRI, subtle strokes will be better seen with more narrowly windowed DWI/ADC images than on preset windows. Considering changing the window and level dynamically for new anatomic region during your search process.

One way to know that a view is well windowed is if the background normal tissue appears mid-grey and grainy. When even background noise is visible, discreet lesions will be much more obvious. As with other strategies aim at improving lesion conspicuity, optimized viewing allows for faster scrolling while maintaining sensitivity.

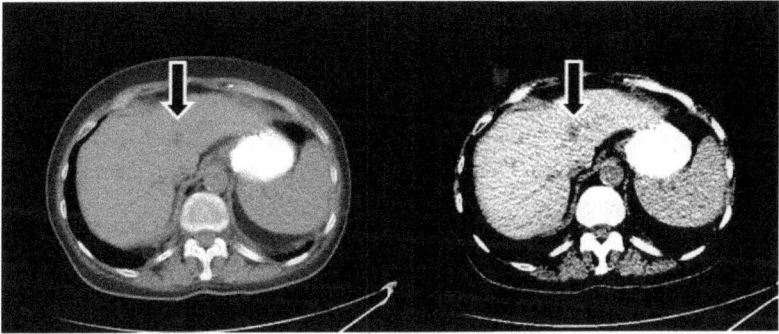

Figure: Example of a subtle liver lesion (arrows) on noncontrast CT of the abdomen, which is much better seen with optimized windowing. Greater conspicuity facilitates faster visual inspection and improves detection of the finding.

Use 3-D overlays and subtraction images whenever possible

Some MPR viewers allow for three-dimensional co-registration of image stacks for rapid comparison. Another tool can produce subtraction images. These functions can be much more efficient than linked or side-by-side scrolling of image stacks. Evaluation using overlayed or subtracted images can also improve detection of subtle lesions, particularly on a background of extensive abnormality.

In our PACS (Visage), images are overlaid within an MPR viewer by clicking and dragging one image stack into viewer with the *left* mouse button, followed by clicking and dragging the second image stack onto the first stack with the *right* mouse button. A special function ("Automatic Registration," which can be assigned to a hotkey) aligns the images. The view can then be smoothly transitioned between the image stacks with a slide bar or toggled with a hotkey ("Toggle Primary"). The images seen with the slide bar pulled to the left correspond with those dragged with the left click; images seen with the slide bar on the right correspond with those dragged with the right click. If warranted, another tool ("Subtract Baseline Phase") can be used to subtract the right-sided images from the left-sided images.

Of note, these functions can be used to compare image stacks from the same study (e.g., differing contrast phases, MRI sequences, or acquisitions) or between differing studies. Co-registration is possible between differing modalities, such as between CT and MRI. Potential uses include assessing for changes in size of brain lesions, ventricular configuration, and intracranial hemorrhage, even across modalities. Despite potential limitations from motion in body imaging, in many cases, co-registration offers highly effective comparison of pulmonary nodules, solid organ lesions, and osseous abnormality.

Production of subtraction images facilitates detection of subtle enhancement and distinguishes enhancement from blood/calcium on CT and from intrinsic T1 hyperintensity on MRI. Subtraction of a prior study from the current facilities detection of otherwise very subtle changes, which may escape notice if using only side-by-side viewing. The ability to subtract between an arbitrary pair of image sets at the workstation (without requiring the aid of technologists) can enhance work efficiency in many scenarios.

Co-registration and subtraction are such powerful tools that we use them for almost all cases in which there are amenable image stacks. These techniques can be combined with dynamic slice thickness changes, toggling between AvIP, MinIP, and MIP, overlapping slices, and manual re-windowing to even further enhance lesion conspicuity. We highly recommend that radiologists with access to these capabilities become familiar with their use.

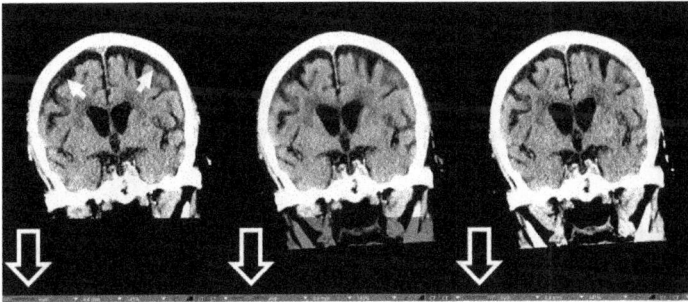

Figure: Comparison using 3-D co-registered images facilitates detection of new/increasing subdural collections, possibly traumatic effusions or chronic subdural hematomas (small arrows) in this patient with trauma. A slide bar (large arrows) smoothly transitions between views of the current (left) and prior (right) studies.

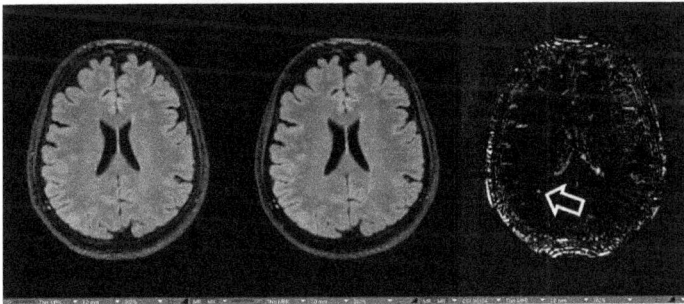

Figure: Subtraction of a prior study (middle) from the current (right) facilitates detection of a very subtle new T2/FLAIR hyperintense white matter lesion (right, arrow) in a patient with multiple sclerosis.

Where relevant, use the "all images" stack

For studies without prior imaging or with less complex expected abnormality, it may be efficient to evaluate the entirety of the study by scrolling through a single stack of "all images" rather than by clicking through multiple panels. Another approach is to use the "all images" stack concurrently with an MPR viewer to reconstruct any sub-stacks as needed.

Using the "all images" stack is useful for quickly screening for incidental findings or unexpected findings. This can be done after characterizing known or expected abnormality using conventional viewing panels in PACS. Using the collated stack also assures that all images are reviewed in all reformats provided. A quick scroll though "all images" can alternatively be used to rapidly triage exams or form a global impression of complex cases.

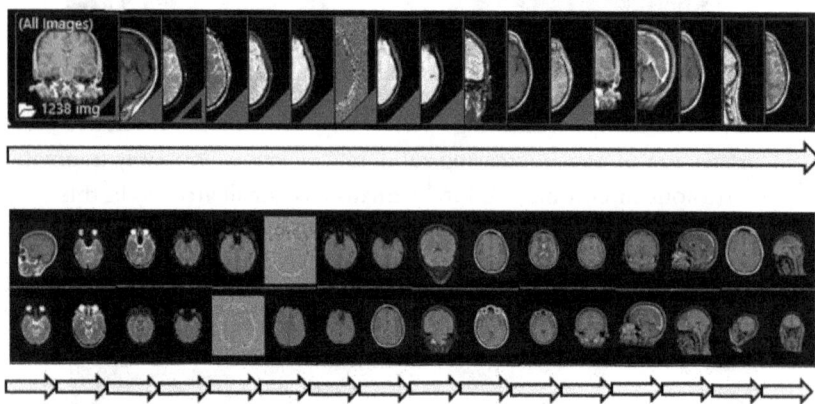

Figure: Example scenario in which using the "all images" stack can be more efficient. Each arrow represents a time when the mouse has to be moved to a new panel, clicked, and scrolled. Additional tabbing through panels in a hanging protocol can also be avoided by using the "all images" stack.

Optimize hanging protocols and viewing panels

Some PACS allow customization of default hanging protocols. Particularly for CT and MRI exams, automated hanging and other preparation of imaging stacks can improve efficiency through minimizing user actions. Even when customization of hanging protocols is not possible within PACS, third-party programs (e.g., AutoHotKey) can be used to automate actions required to hang studies. Use of such tools is further detailed in a later chapter.

When designing a hanging protocol and viewing studies, consider use of small and medium sized viewing panels and minimizing use of whole screen images. Moderate sized panels allow for evaluation of larger regions of anatomy and reduce the need to click though or re-zoom during evaluation.

Consider use of study annotations to remember key findings during exam review

It is common earlier in training to dictate findings as they are seen and later review the entirety of findings to arrive at an impression. Dictation in these cases can serve as a sounding board for diagnostic problem solving.

When reviewing cases prior to dictating or to form a quick gestalt, it can be useful to use PACS annotations such as measurements and arrows to mark important findings. These annotations can be a more efficient means of highlighting key findings than concurrent dictation. Annotations in PACS can also be more helpful than dictating image and series numbers when highlighting findings for referring clinicians or radiologists reading subsequent studies.

In some PACS, annotated images can be easily tabbed through, allowing for efficient review of important findings after the entire case has been assessed.

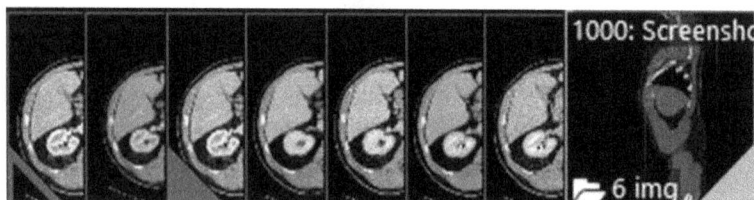

Figure: Example from our PACS in which annotations and screenshots are saved as key images and collected into a dedicated image stack.

Develop search pattern "chunking"

Broadly speaking, "chunking" is a learning process in which smaller pieces of information are combined into meaningful groups to aid with recall or understanding. In radiology, we can use "chunking" to improve the efficiency of search patterns and visual analysis.

Early in residency, trainees develop step-by-step approaches to examine anatomic structures for abnormality. With experience, a radiologist is able to assess larger regions of anatomy simultaneously. For example, rather than looking at each skull base foramen separately, an experienced radiologist may assess the morphology of *collections* of foramina, narrowing their focus to individual structures only if abnormality is detected. Similarly, rather than looking at one rib at a time on chest radiographs or CT, a radiologists may evaluate groups of ribs or multiple adjacent segments simultaneously. This technique improves the ability to process a greater amount visual information at once.

While this "chunking" can develop naturally with experience, it is also possible to consciously develop the skill. During work, consider grouping adjacent structures together for simultaneous evaluation. Potential groupings in general radiology include:

- Multiple neck nodal stations on coronal and sagittal reconstructions of a neck CT.
- Multiple lower lobe pulmonary artery branches laid out on coronal images on chest CTA.
- Grouped sections of small bowel (duodenum, jejunum, and ileum) on coronal reconstructions of abdominopelvic CT.
- Multiple contiguous vertebral bodies, contiguous facets, and adjacent spinous processes on sagittal reconstructions of spine CT.

Finding ideal groupings of anatomic regions will require trial and error, as trying to look at too many structures at once can reduce sensitivity. For each part of one's search pattern, there is likely to be a "sweet spot" of grouping size which can improve efficiency without compromising detection of abnormality. Residency and fellowship are the ideal times to develop these skills, when there is still a safety net of supervision by an attending.

Other techniques described in this chapter facilitate the development of search pattern chunking. Differing image reconstructions within an MPR lay out the anatomy for more intuitive evaluation. Small and medium-sized viewing panels, rather than filing the screen with an image stack, may aid in evaluation of larger groupings of anatomy. Differing intensity projections allow inspection of greater volumes of imaging data per unit time.

Computer aided detection and machine learning

Emerging research suggests that artificial intelligence (AI) based applications can make radiologists faster and more accurate. AI may be most useful when applied to high volume exams and high-risk pathology. For example, AI applications are available to flag cases with suspected acute intracranial hemorrhage on head CT, intracranial large vessel occlusions on head and neck CTA, pulmonary emboli on chest CTA, and suspicious pulmonary nodules on chest radiographs and CT. Research also suggests potential for use in identifying fractures, acute bowel pathology, and many other abnormalities.

Most research has shown that radiologists are more accurate when using AI applications to assist with study analysis. Such tools can reduce mental workload and allow detection of subtle abnormality with less effort. The second set of "machine eyes" can also increase confidence in negative evaluations. This further reassurance for negative cases seems central to the ability of AI applications to improve overall reporting times.

Whether the use of any specific application is worthwhile is likely to depend on many practice-specific factors. However, workflows in the near future of radiology seem likely to involve the management of diverse applications that assist with both detection and triage. These tools, like evolving dictation, PACS, and EHR software, can serve to make us faster, improve accuracy, and increase the value of our contribution to clinical care.

Education and continual improvement

Ideally, onboarding at a new training site or work location includes an introduction to commonly used functions in PACS and any support software. At our program, new residents receive a series of lectures ("bootcamp") including introductions to dictation, PACS, and AI applications. Refreshers with more advanced topics and efficiency-oriented instruction are provided in the middle of the year. Reference sheets for the most valuable shortcuts are disseminated to all trainees and made available within the dictation software as a reference macro. New attending recruits also have access to these materials.

The continual development of PACS-use educational material and onboarding processes is likely to be a high-yield investment for any practice. In any setting, it can be useful to seek out and learn from particularly efficient colleagues. A culture of shared efforts improves the experience for all involved.

High Use Tools
- Change slice thickness - ALT + middle mouse button
- Toggle AvP, MinP, MIP - Shift + T
- 3D viewer / 3D MIP - click bottom of viewer, 2nd panel --> viewer type
- Target (3D localize) - ALT + left mouse key (also useful to find image numbers in all image stack)
- Link scroll (automatic) - L
- Arrow - A
- Window/level - both mouse buttons

3D Overlay
- Go into any MPR viewer
- Drag first study into by clicking and dragging with left mouse button
- Drag second study into by clicking and dragging with left mouse button
- Auto-register (tool with pink and green square)
- Compare by sliding bar back and forth
- Bar toward left = see more of study dragged over with left click
- Bar toward right = see more of study dragged over with right click
- Scroll with keyboard arrow keys while sliding bar with mouse
- Can be combined with thick slices, MIP, invert, 3D visualization, etc.
- Subtraction takes "left" study and subtracts "right" study.
- Can co-register different modalities, e.g. CT/MR/PET, as well as different body parts, e.g. C/T/L spine.

Other useful tools
- Spine labeling - P
- Elliptical ROI - E
- Invert - I
- Angle - G
- Toggle crosshairs - X
- Hide/toggle overlay text - space bar
- Increase overlay text size -- hover over text + control + scroll mouse wheel
- Toggle/hide localizer lines - Q

Avoid losing hanging protocol/study when opening new case (e.g., for consult or correction)
- Control + Shift + S - Save Session As (reload later)
- Right click on Primordial Communicator case
- Open other study through EPIC
- Search in Visage Client--> Right click study --> Open in New Tab/Window

Change view in MPR
- Shift+ A - Anterior view
- Shift+ P - Posterior view
- Shift+ L - Left view
- Shift+ R - Right view
- Shift+ H - Head view
- Shift+ F - Feet view

Customize Hot keys
- Tool palette modification - control + K
- Right click --> bottom right tool
- To see hot keys --> help --> keyboard shortcuts

Useful tools to save:
- Screenshot - S
- Automatic registration - F7
- Subtraction - U
- 3D ROI - W

Powerscribe Shortcuts
- Train phrases that Powerscribe has problems with - highlight + "train that"
- Toggle record - F4 (have to be clicked on Powerscribe)
- Save as draft - F9
- Send report to correction - F10
- Sign report - F12
- Shift + F12 - allows an attending provider to sign a report from a resident's workstation

Figure: Example PACS and dictation guide available to trainees and attendings at our institution.

Selected references

- Shin HJ, Han K, Ryu L, Kim EK. The impact of artificial intelligence on the reading times of radiologists for chest radiographs. NPJ Digital Medicine. 2023 Apr 29;6(1):82.

- Davis MA, Rao B, Cedeno PA, Saha A, Zohrabian VM. Machine Learning and Improved Quality Metrics in Acute Intracranial Hemorrhage by Noncontrast Computed Tomography. Curr Probl Diagn Radiol. 2022 Jul-Aug;51(4):556-561. doi: 10.1067/j.cpradiol.2020.10.007. Epub 2020 Nov 15. PMID: 33243455.

- Fountain SB, Doyle KE. Learning by chunking. Encyclopedia of the Sciences of Learning. 2012:1814-7.

Overview of Effective Reporting

Long H. Tu

Cyrus Safinia

Rahul Hegde

Introduction

Reporting efficiency is often the greatest contributor to differential work speed among radiologists. While some portion of reporting speed is related to the confidence or knowledge base of the radiologist (as well as the type of studies being read) a proportion of the variability also results from differences in reporting style and technique. Perhaps the first step in improving dictation efficiency is moving toward an approach where imaging findings are contextualized with patient management. Further improvement in reporting efficiency can occur through minimizing unnecessary language, improving macros, and adding additional layers of automation.

Description-oriented reporting vs. management-oriented reporting

Residents early in training may develop a dictation approach in which they report each finding in detail as encountered. Once they have completed their search pattern and reported each of the findings in isolation, they look back over the report, and curate the most important items into a separately dictated impression. This can be called a "description-oriented" style of reporting, as what the trainee or radiologist sees drives what they include in the report.

As a radiologist gains experience, their approach to evaluation and reporting may evolve. Experienced radiologists can quickly evaluate the patient as a "whole" and formulate a gestalt that informs how the study can be dictated most efficiently. They can sense what change in management, if any, will occur as a result of that study. Efficient radiologists will then use only as many words as are required to convey the crucial findings supporting the expected change in clinical care. Findings which are not expected to have clinical significance are acknowledged with as few words as possible, if at all. Findings with no significance may alternatively be covered by "catch-all" statements in a template. In some sense, this approach imagines clinical care first, the "impression" second, and how to report "findings" last.

With a more targeted dictation style, less time and effort are required to influence the appropriate course of care. Reports, however, are more readable for referrers and subsequent radiologists. As a caveat, this mode of thinking is most applicable to scenarios where there are a variety of potential reporting approaches. Certain areas in radiology (breast imaging, follow-up of thyroid nodules, etc.) require specific reporting elements, which should be used consistently.

The use of management-oriented reporting requires a knowledge base and understanding of how radiologic findings impact downstream care. It is therefore essential for radiologists, through training and beyond, to engage in learning that will help them be as clinically relevant as possible. For those who by habit "over-describe," switching to management-oriented thinking and dictation can produce marked improvements in efficiency.

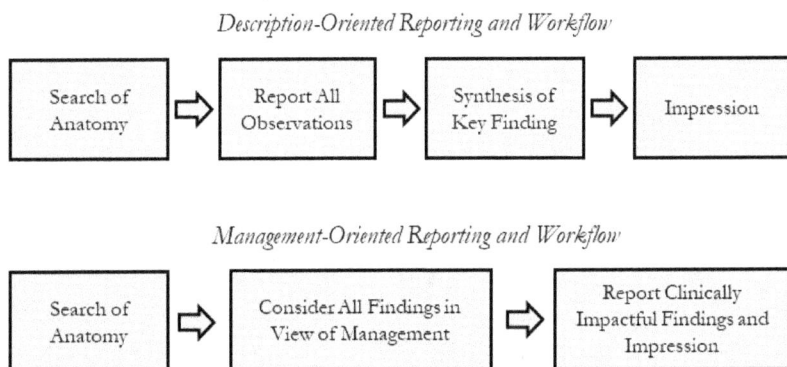

Description-Oriented Reporting and Workflow

Management-Oriented Reporting and Workflow

Figure: Management-oriented vs description-oriented reporting.

Dictation examples

In each of the following examples, imagine free-dictating the length of the report (or at least the abnormal findings). Consider the level of effort involved to complete each style of report or to read this report if one were a referring clinician or a radiologist interpreting a follow-up study. The following examples are for illustrative purposes and do not necessarily represent an ideal or universally preferred means of reporting. Only relevant parts of the reports are shown.

Description-Oriented	Management-Oriented
FINDINGS: There is prominence of the bilateral central pulmonary vasculature and patchy bilateral airspace opacities in a diffuse pattern. There is blunting of the bilateral costophrenic angles, raising the possibility of minimal pleural effusions. The cardiomediastinal silhouette is grossly widened. There is calcification of the aortic arch. The median sternotomy wires are in stable position. There is no acute displaced fracture. There are degenerative changes at the right glenohumeral joint and thoracic spine. There are cholecystectomy clips again noted in the right upper quadrant. **IMPRESSION:** Bilateral patchy airspace opacities as well as small pleural effusions are suggestive of pulmonary edema, aspiration, and/or pneumonia in the appropriate clinical setting.	**FINDINGS:** Patchy bilateral airspace opacities. Questionable/trace bilateral pleural effusions. Enlarged cardiac silhouette. No displaced fracture. Median sternotomy wires and upper abdominal clips. **IMPRESSION:** Patchy airspace opacities suggesting pulmonary edema versus aspiration/pneumonia.

Example: Airspace opacities. In the management-oriented dictation, note the use of noun-phrases, the omission of observations unlikely to impact management, and concise description of other findings. The briefer report is much faster to dictate and understand. Notice how there is virtually the same amount of true "content" in both reports.

Description-Oriented	Management-Oriented
FINDINGS: Redemonstration of surgical staples overlying the right skull vertex. There are changes of prior right craniectomy. Compared with most recent study, a previous drainage catheter along the right subdural space has been removed. There are similar locules of gas along the extra-axial space and scalp. Scalp edema noted. The right holohemispheric subdural hematoma is stable in size, 6mm in thickness when measured similarly. There is stable mass effect and effacement upon the right lateral ventricle compared with prior. No midline shift. No new intracranial hemorrhage is seen. Atherosclerotic calcifications are again noted in the bilateral carotid siphons and left vertebral artery. Hypodensity in the left temporal pole measuring 1.5 cm could represent a left middle cranial fossa arachnoid cyst, similar to prior. No abnormality is identified within the visualized orbits. Paranasal sinuses and mastoid air cells are unremarkable. **IMPRESSION:** Status post removal of a drainage catheter along the right frontotemporal craniectomy site. Stable right holohemispheric subdural hematoma measuring 6mm in thickness. Redemonstrated scalp edema.	**FINDINGS:** Interval removal of subdural drain. Otherwise, similar postsurgical changes. Stable 6 mm thickness right subdural hematoma. Similar local mass effect. No midline shift. No new hemorrhage. Similar probable left middle cranial fossa arachnoid cyst. No orbital abnormality seen. Paranasal sinuses and mastoid air cells are unremarkable. **IMPRESSION:** Stable 6 mm thickness subdural hematoma status post drain removal.

Example: CT after removal of a subdural drain. There is no need to extensively describe postsurgical changes which are known, expected, or which have been previously characterized. In this case, the clinicians want to know if there has been any acute or unexpected change after a drain has been removed. As long as a radiologist has conveyed that there has not been such a change, the key objective is accomplished. Consider how much easier it is to obtain critical information skimming the briefer report.

Description-Oriented	Management-Oriented
FINDINGS: There is a stable 2.5 cm right hepatic hypodensity compatible with simple cyst. There are two hypodensities too small to characterize in the left lobe of the liver, similar to prior. The gallbladder and bile ducts are unremarkable. The pancreas is unremarkable. Redemonstrated borderline splenomegaly measuring up to 13 cm. There are two left sided nonobstructive renal calculi measuring 2 mm and 5mm respectively. No hydronephrosis. There is stranding of the mesenteric fat surrounding diverticula at the sigmoid colon. There is no evidence of perforation. No discrete collection to suggest abscess is seen. There is no bowel obstruction. There are atherosclerotic calcifications of the abdominal aorta without aneurysm. There is no adenopathy in the abdomen or pelvis. There is no free air. There is no ascites. There are degenerative changes in the lumbar spine comprised of endplate osteophytosis, sclerosis, cystic change, and disc-space narrowing. There are no acute fractures or aggressive osseous lesions. **IMPRESSION:** Inflammation around diverticula at the sigmoid colon is consistent with acute diverticulitis. No evidence of abscess or frank perforation.	**FINDINGS:** Hepatic cysts and hypodensities too small to characterize. Gallbladder and pancreas are unremarkable. Borderline splenomegaly. Nonobstructive renal calculi up to 5mm. Inflammation surrounding sigmoid diverticula. No collection. No bowel obstruction. No pneumoperitoneum, ascites, or adenopathy. No acute or aggressive osseous lesion. **IMPRESSION:** Acute uncomplicated sigmoid diverticulitis.

Example: Acute diverticulitis. Note the overall reduction in words that hold no meaningful or management-changing content. Findings that do not impact care (such as hepatic cysts) need not be measured or described at length. A constellation of findings that has only one explanatory diagnosis, such as acute diverticulitis in this case, can be summarized in the impression by simply naming the diagnosis. The resultant dictation is much easier to read, even with a narrative format. Longer or more complex cases may be better reported using a "structured" reporting style.

Consider structured reporting where applicable

A growing body of research suggests that referring clinicians prefer structured reports. Structured reports are more likely to be complete, readable, and address the questions of clinicians. Even if requiring a similar (or even greater) amount of time for dictation, structured reports may improve downstream efficiency for later radiologists reading follow-up studies and potentially reduces inquiries for clarification from clinicians. A structured reporting format may aid in reinforcing search patterns, especially for trainees and less experienced radiologists. Structured reports may also improve the efficiency of research and quality improvement projects, due to more predictable formatting.

Freeform Report Example	Structured Report Example
FINDINGS: Hepatic hypodensities too small to characterize. Status post cholecystectomy. The pancreas is edematous, with surrounding inflammatory changes. No differential parenchymal enhancement. No peripancreatic collections seen. Spleen is unremarkable. Renal cysts and hypodensities too small to characterize. Nonobstructive renal calculi measuring up to 3mm. Bladder is unremarkable. The appendix is unremarkable. No bowel obstruction. Colonic diverticulosis without evidence of acute diverticulitis. No evidence of venous thrombosis, active arterial hemorrhage, or pseudoaneurysm. No pneumoperitoneum, ascites, or adenopathy. No acute or aggressive osseous lesion. **IMPRESSION:** Acute interstitial edematous pancreatitis. No peripancreatic fluid collections.	**FINDINGS:** LIVER: Hepatic hypodensities too small to characterize. GALLBLADDER/BILIARY: Status post cholecystectomy. PANCREAS: Edematous, with surrounding inflammatory changes. No differential parenchymal enhancement. No peripancreatic collection. SPLEEN: Unremarkable. KIDNEYS: Cysts and hypodensities too small to characterize. Nonobstructive calculi measuring up to 3mm. BLADDER/PELVIS: Unremarkable. BOWEL: Appendix is unremarkable. No bowel obstruction. Colonic diverticulosis without evidence of acute diverticulitis. VESSELS: No evidence of venous thrombosis, active arterial hemorrhage, or pseudoaneurysm. PERITONEUM/LYMPH NODES: No pneumoperitoneum, ascites, or adenopathy. OSSEOUS STRUCTURES: No acute or aggressive osseous lesion. **IMPRESSION:** Acute interstitial edematous pancreatitis. No peripancreatic fluid collections.

Example: Acute pancreatitis. Imagine you're a clinician concerned that the patient may have complications of acute pancreatitis. Even with efficient reporting practices, reports in freeform or paragraph format can be difficult to scan for information about specific organ systems. Key findings may be buried in paragraphs, without visual cues to assist quick identification. Note how it can be easier to locate the description of pancreatic abnormalities and pertinent negative vascular findings in the structured example.

Triage of dictation effort improves efficiency

Strategic allocation of effort to cases of differing complexity can improve work efficiency. As a general principle, it can be useful to aim for reports that are as concise as possible, while still containing as much detail as necessary to guide the highest quality of care. The goal should be to modulate the level of effort (and reporting detail) to what is necessary for each case.

In most practices, "negative" (or stable) exams represent the largest proportion of overall volume. The speed at which these exams are interpreted plays a large role in overall efficiency. The same idea applies to non-diagnostic studies. Once confidently categorized – after equally careful inspection – negative, stable, and non-diagnostic cases should be reported with as minimal an approach as possible.

Even most positive exams will be comprised of straightforward findings and pathology. Having "canned" phrases ready for such cases can make them as easy to report as negative ones.

The subset of cases in radiology that requires deeper thought are those with complex or uncommon pathology. While it is wasteful to dedicate inordinate effort to negative or straightforward studies, it is also poor form to rush through cases where subtle distinctions can impact patient care. Greater discussion of differential possibilities and follow-up recommendations can be valuable and improve patient outcomes in challenging cases. Be ready to slow down when it is required.

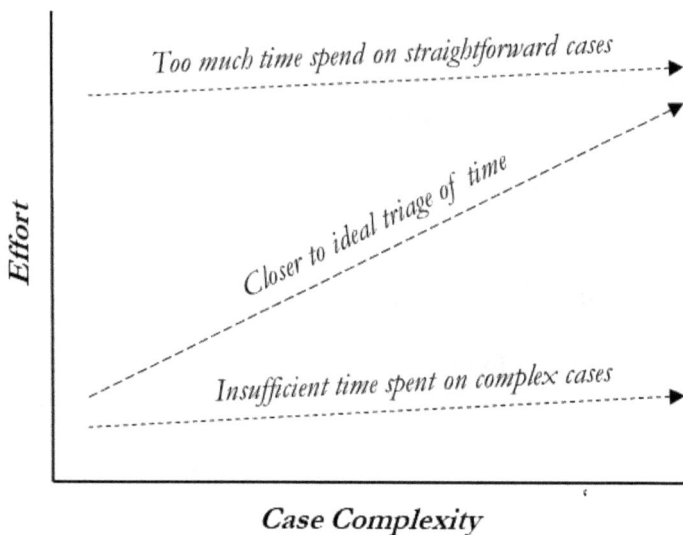

Figure: Conceptual graph of modulating effort to case complexity.

Unnecessarily Detailed	Sufficient
FINDINGS: The patient is status post interval reduction of the previously noted fractures of the distal radial and ulnar diaphyses. The fracture fragments are now in anatomic alignment. Casting material obscures evaluation of the fine osseous details and soft tissues. No new fractures or dislocation identified. There are similar mild degenerative changes at the ulnotrochlear articulation. There is similar soft tissue swelling about the forearm. No radiopaque foreign body is identified. **IMPRESSION:** Status post reduction of the previously described distal radius and ulnar fractures with improved, anatomic alignment.	**FINDINGS/IMPRESSION:** Anatomic alignment status post reduction. No new acute finding.

Example: Post-reduction radiograph. Imagine that the report of a preceding radiograph had already described the fractures and other anatomy in sufficient detail to guide management. The role of the radiologist, with the follow-up study, is to assess post-reduction alignment. In rare cases, a new abnormality may be seen. A brief report is sufficient if it answers these implied questions.

Reports that are very brief (e.g., 1-2 sentences), may not require a separate impression according to ACR guidelines. Local practice policies may impact the appropriateness of combining the findings and impression, or omitting a separate impression.

Insufficiently Detailed	Sufficiently Detailed
FINDINGS: (Visceral findings omitted)	**FINDINGS:** (Visceral findings omitted)
OSSEOUS STRUCTURES: Increasing diffuse spinal and osseous pelvic metastases, the largest at L2. No acute fracture.	OSSEOUS STRUCTURES: Increasing diffuse osseous metastases, the largest at L2. Cortical breakthrough of the posterior cortex with abnormal soft tissue producing moderate encroachment on the spinal canal. No acute fracture.
IMPRESSION: Increasing osseus metastases.	**IMPRESSION:** Increasing osseous metastases with posterior extension into the spinal canal at L2. Consider MRI with and without contrast for further evaluation.

Example: Progressive osseous metastases. There is a fine balance between brevity and completeness. In some cases, additional details can genuinely impact management. In this example, noting that a dominant metastatic lesion involves not just the vertebra, but also the spinal canal, can alter further evaluation and management. Of course, knowing what findings impact care requires broader medical knowledge and, in some cases, discussion with clinical colleagues.

Insufficiently Detailed	Sufficiently Detailed
INDICATION: Shortness of breath. COPD and HIV/AIDS not on HAART.	**INDICATION:** Shortness of breath. COPD and HIV/AIDS not on HAART.
FINDINGS: Worsening patchy bilateral airspaces opacities in an upper lobe predominance, more focal and prominent on the right. No pleural effusion or pneumothorax seen. The cardiomediastinal silhouette is normal. No acute osseous abnormality seen.	**FINDINGS:** Worsening patchy bilateral airspaces opacities in an upper lobe predominance, with mass-like appearance on the right. No pleural effusion or pneumothorax seen. The cardiomediastinal silhouette is normal. No acute osseous abnormality seen.
IMPRESSION: Increasing patchy bilateral airspace opacities.	**IMPRESSION:** 1. Increasing airspace opacities, suspicious for aspiration/pneumonia, including opportunistic infections. 2. A region with more mass-like appearance in the right upper lobe raises the possibility of other underlying lesion, such as neoplasm. Recommend further evaluation by CT.

Example: Nonspecific airspace opacities. A patient with history of HIV/AIDS and COPD is at risk for uncommon pathologies, including opportunistic infection, as well as common and uncommon neoplasia. The insufficiently detailed report may not only fall below the standard of care for such a patient, but also instigate a call for clarification of what the airspace opacities might represent. It is good practice to include differential considerations when they would be helpful. Merely repeating the imaging finding in the impression leaves much room for confusion.

Summary concepts

Reporting efficiency is perhaps the greatest contributor to overall work speed. To facilitate a transition to management-oriented reporting, it can be helpful to keep the following questions in mind for each exam:

- What change in care will result from this study?
- What is the most concise, yet complete impression that motivates that change?
- What else, if anything, does the clinician want to know from this study?
- What is the most efficient description of findings that justifies the impression?

In the following chapters we will consider specific habits, strategies, and macro-based optimizations that can assist with efficient reporting. Reducing the mental demands of reporting can free attention for other tasks where we positively impact patient care.

Efficient Dictation Tips

Long H. Tu

Quoc-Huy Ly

Rahul Hegde

Introduction

Specific dictation habits may impact overall efficiency. As much of the content and wording of each report as possible should be crucial for guiding management, with little or no filler. In this chapter, we review specific habits for free-dictation that can be modified to achieve this aim. Macro-based efficiencies follow in later chapters.

Minimize use of declarative phrases

Phrases such as *"there is," "is noted," "is again noted,"* and *"redemonstrated"* are generally unnecessary to convey meaning. Instead of using declarative sentences, consider merely listing the finding as a noun-phrase. "Demonstrated" and "redemonstrated" are particularly inefficient due to their vagueness and number of syllables. Instead of saying that a finding is "redemonstrated," consider stating clearly whether there has been change compared to prior.

In some settings, this style of reporting is considered too brief and may not be appropriate. In acute, emergency, or otherwise high-volume settings, clinicians may appreciate brevity. Less can be more, depending on who is expected to read the report.

Instead of:	Consider:
A hepatic hypodensity too small to characterize is again noted.	Hepatic hypodensity too small to characterize.
There is a stable 2.3 cm right renal mass.	Stable 2.3 cm right renal mass.
Left subdural hematoma is again noted, measuring 2.6 cm in thickness.	Stable 2.6 cm subdural hematoma.
There are redemonstrated hepatic metastases, measuring up to 3.5 cm, stable compared to prior.	Stable hepatic metastases, measuring up to 3.5 cm.
L5-S1 pars defects are present.	L5-S1 pars defects.

Minimize use of perceptive terms

Similar to declarative phrases, terms of perception such as "is seen," "observed," and "visualized" add little value to reports. If a finding is stated, it can be presumed to have been visualized. In some cases, if a study is limited, or if a finding is equivocal, terms of perception can be useful to indicate the level of confidence in an observation. Terms of perception can also be helpful as default wording in templates where regions of anatomy are only partially imaged or incompletely evaluated. However, excessive use in free dictation is likely to reduce reporting efficiency.

Instead of:	Consider:
A spinal hemangioma is again visualized, similar to prior.	Similar spinal hemangioma.
Postsurgical changes of prior cholecystectomy are seen.	Prior cholecystectomy.
A large joint effusion is observed.	Large joint effusion.
There are surgical clips seen in the right axillary region.	Right axillary surgical clips.

Use brief phrases to indicate stability

The words "stable," "similar," and "unchanged" are concise options and preferred to phrases such as "unchanged compared to prior" or "without significant interval change." If the comparison is clear from the report header and context, then there is no need to name the specific comparison exam. In some cases, such as when change from prior does not impact care, comparison can be omitted entirely.

There will be some cases where "stable" is preferred, such as in certain cancer staging criteria (e.g., RECIST), where "stable" has a specific meaning. There are other scenarios where "stable" may be misleading. Metastatic disease might be more carefully described as either "similar" or "stable in appearance," if the interval of follow up is too short to expect perceptible change, yet progressive disease is possible.

"Similar" can also be used as a more generic term, if there are inherent limitations or caveats related to short interval of follow-up or differences in technique (e.g., comparing the size of a brain lesion between MRI and CT.)

Instead of:	Consider:
Reticulation and bronchiectasis at the right lung base are unchanged compared to prior study.	Unchanged right basilar reticulation and bronchiectasis.
Left occipital encephalomalacia is similar in appearance compared to prior MRI, though exact comparison is somewhat limited by differences in technique.	Similar left occipital encephalomalacia.
No significant change in 2.0 cm left frontal meningioma compared to remote prior CT study in 2009.	Stable 2.0 cm left frontal meningioma.
Stable 1.5 cm right renal cyst.	Right renal cyst.
Incidental hepatic hypodensities too small to characterize appear stable compared to remote prior study in 2007.	Hepatic hypodensities too small to characterize.

> **Avoid describing incidental, expected, or incompletely characterized observations that do not impact care**

Just because one makes an observation does not mean it is necessary to mention it. Many observations do not change management and could be omitted.

Instead of:	Consider:
There is impacted cerumen in the bilateral external auditory canals. (On a head CT for trauma.)	(Nothing.)
There are degenerative changes of the acromioclavicular joint and glenohumeral joint. (On a chest radiograph for shortness of breath in an 80-year-old male patient.)	"No acute osseous abnormality." (Or nothing.)
There are multilevel degenerative changes in the lumbar spine manifested by endplate spurring, sclerosis, cystic change, disc height loss, and vacuum phenomenon, worst at L4-L5. No high-grade osseous encroachment on the spinal canal. No fractures seen. (On a CT of the abdomen and pelvis for abdominal pain.)	"No acute osseous abnormality."
There is scattered atherosclerotic calcification of the abdominal aorta and its branches. No aortic aneurysm is seen. (On non-contrast CT of the abdomen and pelvis for flank pain in a 75-year-old patient with known coronary artery disease.)	"No aortic aneurysm."

Avoid describing variant anatomy that will not change management

Uncommonly variant anatomy may sometimes impact care. For example, brisk arterial hemorrhage in the setting of trauma from a "corona mortis" variant pelvic artery should be described. Variant aortic arch anatomy should be described if thrombectomy for stroke is expected. Residents early in training may benefit from describing variants to demonstrate knowledge or practice recognition. In most other cases, these variants need not be mentioned.

Instead of:	Consider:
There is an azygous fissure and lobe.	(Nothing.)
There is common origin of the brachiocephalic trunk and the left common carotid artery, a "bovine" configuration.	(Nothing.)
There is a diminutive left P1 segment of the posterior cerebellar artery, with prominent ipsilateral posterior communicating artery, suggesting a persistent fetal pattern of circulation.	(Nothing.)
There is a Reidel hepatic lobe.	(Nothing.)
There is a septum pellucidum.	(Nothing.)

> **Minimize description of findings that should already be clinically apparent or which are not well assessed with imaging**

This guidance applies most commonly to soft tissue swelling, lacerations, and other superficial abnormalities not well evaluated by imaging (usually radiographs). It can be unnecessary to mention that the soft tissues are normal or "unremarkable" on radiographs. In some cases, such statements can seem misguided, when there are obvious abnormalities seen clinically but not radiographically. It is better to provide pertinent negatives such as "no radiopaque foreign body," "no joint effusion," or "no evidence of subcutaneous gas."

Instead of:	Consider:
The soft tissues are unremarkable. (On most radiographs of the extremities.)	(Nothing.)
There is marked soft tissue swelling about the ankle. (When such a finding should already be clinically relevant.)	(Nothing.)
There is a right frontal scalp edema. No calvarial fracture.	No calvarial fracture.

Minimize descriptions for findings with only one likely explanation

While the findings section should generally only contain "objective" observations, radiologists commonly include straightforward interpretations to avoid excessive description. This approach can minimize unnecessary dictation, though should only be used when an appearance has only one possible interpretation.

Instead of:	Consider:
There is a 2.3 cm right frontal convexity extra-axial homogeneously enhancing mass with a few foci of internal calcification and a dural tail. There is similar thickening and remodeling of the adjacent calvarium. This finding is stable compared to prior.	Stable 2.3 cm right frontal meningioma.
Stable 1.2 cm low density lesion (<10 HU) at the right adrenal gland, previously characterized as an adenoma on multiple prior studies dating back to 2009.	Stable 1.2 cm right adrenal adenoma.
There has been interval suboccipital craniectomy for resection of the left cerebellar mass, more fully characterized on prior MRI. Minimal foci of pneumocephalus, as expected given short interval since surgery. Adjacent scalp edema is likely related to post-operative state.	Expected postsurgical changes of suboccipital craniectomy.
There is a 2.0 cm homogenous, non-enhancing left renal lesion with imperceptible walls, no nodular/mass-like internal components, and Hounsfield units <10.	Left renal cyst.
Diffuse low attenuation of the liver likely represents steatotic change.	Hepatic steatosis.

Avoid wording which is unnecessarily specific

Just because something is true does not mean that it needs to be mentioned. Findings can be described using a more generalized or "broad strokes" approach, when details do not have clinical impact.

Instead of:	Consider:	Notes:
A 2.0 cm probable hemangioma is seen in segment 3 of the liver.	2.0 cm probable hepatic hemangioma.	Location is unlikely to be relevant to care for a lesion which does not requirement intervention.
Similar encephalomalacia at the right superior frontal gyrus, operculum, and gyrus rectus. Associated ex vacuo dilatation of the lateral ventricle.	Similar regions of right cerebral encephalomalacia.	Except where it changes management or specifically explains a presentation, old strokes do not need to be described with great detail. Ex vacuo phenomenon is good to recognize, but does not alter management aside from helping distinguish volume loss from hydrocephalus.
Cholecystectomy clips project at the right upper quadrant. (On a chest radiograph without known prior history.)	Surgical clips project at the upper abdomen.	Not all surgical clips in the right upper quadrant, are related to prior cholecystectomy. (Partial hepatectomy, adrenalectomy, and retroperitoneal mass resection are uncommon possibilities.) Specific description is unnecessary and introduces possibility of error, especially if the history is not known.

Avoid measurements which do not impact care or improve the understanding of pathology

---

This is a more specific example of avoiding descriptors that do not affect management. Note that in some circumstances, such as for staging of specific malignancies, measurements in multiple axes will be required. Recognize which (largest, smallest, etc.) dimension of adenopathy is relevant to staging or description at differing anatomic sites.

Instead of:	Consider:	Notes:
Left renal cyst measures 1.2 cm.	Left renal cyst.	Simple renal cysts rarely impact management, unless so large that they produce mass effect/symptoms.
An incidental right upper lobe pulmonary nodule measures up to 6 mm. A left upper lobe pulmonary nodule measures up to 4 mm. Smaller solid nodules measuring up to 3 mm are also noted.	Scattered solid pulmonary nodules measure up to 6 mm.	Fleischer criteria (recommendations for follow up of incidental pulmonary nodules) depends only on the dimension of the largest pulmonary nodule.
Right level II cervical lymph nodes measure 4.2 x 2.4 x 1.4 cm and 2.6 x 2.0 x 1.4 cm. *(In patient with recurrent head and neck cancer.)*	Right level II cervical adenopathy measuring up to 4.2 cm.	Head and neck cancer is staged based on largest nodal dimension according to the most recent AJCC guidelines (at time of writing). The remaining dimensions generally do not impact management.
Right hilar adenopathy measures up to 2.6 x 2.5 x 2.3 cm, stable compared to prior.	Stable 2.3 cm right hilar adenopathy.	Thoracic lymph nodes are measured in short axis.

Consider annotating images in PACS rather than dictating image numbers

In some PACS, key images can be saved and annotated to guide clinicians and radiologists who may need to review the study at a later time. Generally, using PACS functions to skip to key findings or looking for annotations within a study is easier and faster than scrolling to specific image numbers. Dictating image numbers may also take longer than annotating key images. The use of either approach will depend on the needs and preferences of each practice setting. Future advances in software integration may allow automated import of image numbers to the report with annotation, reducing this potential burden.

Instead of:	Consider (along with PACS annotations):
Increasing size of pulmonary nodules measuring up to 7mm such as on series 3 images 230, 275, and 290.	Increasing size of pulmonary nodules measuring up to 7mm.
Extravasation of contrast at the colonic anastomosis (series 901, image 401).	Extravasation of contrast at the colonic anastomosis.

> **Avoid including observations in the impression which are unlikely to change management or explain the patient's presentation**

Findings which are not actionable/explanatory can be kept in the body of the report. These remain searchable in the unlikely event that they are later found to be relevant.

Instead of:	Consider:
IMPRESSION: 1. Non-obstructive renal calculi measure up to 3mm. No hydronephrosis. 2. Left renal cyst.	IMPRESSION: No evidence of acute abnormality in the abdomen and pelvis.
IMPRESSION: 1. Acute fracture of L3 with displacement of fracture fragments into the spinal canal. 2. Spinal hemangiomas. 3. Small hiatal hernia.	IMPRESSION: Acute burst fracture of L3, with retropulsed fragments producing severe spinal stenosis.

Avoid excessive description of findings in the impression section

The impression section of a report should be ordered by importance or acuity. Generally, the impression section should be composed of diagnoses or clinical terminology representing a synthesis of the radiologic findings. Specific radiologic signs and findings need not necessarily be included. In some cases, particularly when a constellation of findings has a differential, it can be useful to provide the findings which support the list of considerations.

Keep in mind the question that is most important to answer for the referring clinician. Try to answer that question as early in the impression and with as efficient language as possible.

Instead of:	Consider:
IMPRESSION: Inflammatory changes about the appendix compatible with acute appendicitis. No collection or evidence of perforation.	IMPRESSION: Acute uncomplicated appendicitis.
IMPRESSION: Status post left frontal craniotomy for resection of mass lesion. Similar minimal pneumocephalus and scalp edema. No evidence of new intracranial hemorrhage, mass effect, or acute ischemic infarct.	IMPRESSION: Expected postoperative appearance. No unexpected acute findings.
IMPRESSION: Status post posterior decompression and instrumented fusion spanning L3-S1. The hardware is in expected configuration without evidence of failure. No evidence of compression fracture or traumatic listhesis.	IMPRESSION: No evidence of acute osseous abnormality or hardware failure.

Summary

It is still common for radiologists to describe findings such as cysts and hypodensities in solid organs which are unlikely to impact care. Many findings which we routinely include in reports could conceivably be considered part of the range of "normal" aging, including some degree of skeletal degenerative change or brain parenchymal volume loss. At the time of writing, it is still common to report measurements of normal structures on ultrasound studies (often in three dimensions) despite no impact on clinical care. Perhaps in the future, advances in reporting standards can minimize efficiency drag from non-actionable observations. There are many areas for collective improvement.

A recap of the approaches in this chapter:

1. Minimize use of declarative phrases.
2. Minimize use of perceptive terms.
3. Use brief phrases to indicate stability.
4. Avoid describing incidental, expected, or incompletely characterized observations that do not impact care.
5. Avoid describing variant anatomy that will not change management.
6. Minimize description of findings that should already be clinically apparent or which are not well assessed with imaging.
7. Minimize descriptions for findings with only one likely explanation.
8. Avoid wording which is unnecessarily specific.
9. Avoid measurements which do not impact care or improve the understanding of pathology.
10. Consider annotating images in PACS rather than dictating imaging numbers.
11. Avoid including observations in the impression which are unlikely to change management or explain the patient's presentation.
12. Avoid excessive description of findings in the impression section.

Selected references

- Hartung MP, Bickle IC, Gaillard F, Kanne JP. How to create a great radiology report. RadioGraphics. 2020 Oct;40(6):1658-70.
- McGrath AL, Dodelzon K, Awan OA, Said N, Bhargava P. Optimizing radiologist productivity and efficiency: Work smarter, not harder. European Journal of Radiology. 2022 Oct 1;155:110131.
- Hall FM. Language of the radiology report: primer for residents and wayward radiologists. American Journal of Roentgenology. 2000 Nov;175(5):1239-42.
- Wallis A, McCoubrie P. The radiology report—are we getting the message across?. Clinical radiology. 2011 Nov 1;66(11):1015-22.
- Langlotz CP. The Radiology Report: A Guide to Thoughtful Communication for Radiologists and Other Medical Professionals. CreateSpace Independent Publishing Platform. 2015. ISBN: 978-1515174080.

Macro Optimization

Long H. Tu

Peter Hung

E. Brooke Schrickel

Introduction

Beyond efficient free-dictation, optimization of dictation macros and templates can provide further improvements in work speed. In this chapter, which refers to the most common dictation software, PowerScribe, we provide examples of macros ("AutoTexts") which are useful in general radiology. These examples are available in an online repository, which is more fully described in a following chapter.

Macro cloning, creation, and use

Ideally, all radiology residents are introduced to macro use early in training. PowerScribe allows the "cloning" (copying) of macros from other users. This can be an efficient means of providing new trainees a library of useful tools for reporting. PowerScribe also allows the creation of systems macros, which are often used to auto-populate templates with differing exam codes. Systems macros can be a useful means of introducing trainees to standardized and efficient reporting language, as they are immediately available to all users, without requiring import into a personal profile. Onboarding processes may be helpful to introduce trainees to the most valuable macros for their early rotations.

Radiologists in general have personal preferences in reporting style. For any individual, all phrases that are repeated commonly should be condensed into personalized macros. PowerScribe has a function where new macros can be created by highlighting any text in a report and saying "macro that." This can be a very helpful tool, which we recommend applying liberally.

A few miscellaneous functions related to macro use are relevant to mention here. The voice command for calling a macro can be changed between "macro," "PowerScribe," or "AutoText." Using "macro" may be advantageous, as it has the fewest syllabus. In many cases, it is not necessary to say the whole name of a macro, only the first set of syllables unique to that macro. For example, a macro named "old brain" can be called by saying "macro old" instead of "macro old brain" so long as there are no other macro that start with "old."

During both training and practice, pressure to keep up with clinical work can crowd out investment in activities that produce greater long-term efficiency. Macro creation and refinement is chief among such activities. It can therefore be useful for individual radiologists to set aside specific times for macro development and macro-related training.

Macros for common findings

Macros may be created for common incidental findings, nonspecific observations, and postsurgical changes. Below are examples of macros which we commonly use in general and emergency radiology. Any practice setting is likely to have a similar collection of high-yield short phrases which could be saved as macros.

Macro Name	Macro Text
Old brain	Scattered regions of periventricular and subcortical white matter hypodensity are nonspecific, but likely related to chronic small vessel ischemia.
Atrophy	The ventricles and sulci are symmetric and prominent in size, likely reflecting diffuse parenchymal volume loss.
NPH	Ventriculomegaly slightly out of proportion to sulcal prominence is nonspecific and may reflect a pattern of parenchymal volume loss. However, normal pressure hydrocephalus may also be considered in the appropriate clinical setting.
Lens	Status post bilateral lens replacement.
Big PA	The main pulmonary artery is enlarged, which may be seen in pulmonary hypertension.
Diverticulosis	Colonic diverticulosis without evidence of acute diverticulitis.
Cholelithiasis	Cholelithiasis without CT evidence of acute cholecystitis.
Appendectomy	The appendix is not visualized, compatible with documented prior appendectomy.
No failure	No evidence of hardwire failure/complication.
No radiopaque	No radiopaque foreign body seen.
Dimensions	(AP x TV x CC)

Macros for common hedges

Commonly repeated phrases may include hedges for studies that are technically limited or other cases where only incomplete evaluation is possible. These caveats are good candidates for macro creation, particularly because hedges are often lengthy. Below are common hedges which may be used in an acute and emergency imaging.

Macro Name	Macro Text
Exclude	Superimposed infectious etiology would have to be excluded clinically.
Motion	Motion degraded study. Subtle abnormality may not be detected.
Low lung volumes	The lung volumes are low, producing crowding of the lower lung markings and prominence of the cardiomediastinal silhouette.
Limited PE	The more peripheral pulmonary artery branches are poorly evaluated due to streak/mixing artifact. Emboli cannot be entirely excluded at these sites.
No brain mets	No large intracranial mass identified. Please note that noncontrast CT is of low sensitivity for brain metastases. Recommend further evaluation via MRI with and without contrast as clinically warranted.
Stroke hedge	If the patient has new focal neurologic symptoms and/or other findings concerning for an acute infarct, consider further evaluation with MRI.
Seizure hedge	Please note that noncontrast CT is of limited sensitivity in evaluation of seizure etiology. If there is persistent clinical concern, further evaluation with MRI would be more sensitive.
Torsion hedge	Please note that with increased size of the ovary, torsion-detorsion phenomenon cannot be entirely excluded on ultrasound, even with normal arterial flow and resistive index.

Fetal hedge	Please note, this study was performed in the emergency room setting only for the indicated reason. Detailed imaging/evaluation of the fetal anatomy was not performed. Follow-up obstetric evaluation for this purpose may be pursued as clinically warranted.
Breast hedge	Please note this study was done in the emergent setting only for the evaluation of acute pathologies. Evaluation for breast neoplasm would have to be performed at a dedicated breast center.

Macros with merge fields

Other macros ("modules") composed of basic report components can aid in macro creation or on-the-fly editing of reports with non-standard formatting. "Merge fields" which contain DICOM info or other metadata such as ordering provider name, study timestamp, or current time can be used to document information such as time-sensitive communication with clinicians. Specialized custom Merge fields, which can be created through collaboration with IT or third-party vendors, allow for deeper PACS and EHR integration. These custom fields can extract information such as contrast dose and dates of comparison studies. They may also be leveraged to automate notifying clinician of critical results (described in a later chapter).

Macro Name	Macro Text
Header	[Procedure Name] PROVIDED INDICATION: [Indication] COMPARISON: [Comparison Dates]
Comparison	COMPARISON: [Comparison Dates]
Contrast	IV CONTRAST: [Contrast Agent and Dose]
History	ADDITIONAL HISTORY OBTAINED FROM ELECTRONIC MEDICAL RECORD: [Other Comments]
Acuity	Radiology Notify System Classification: [Acuity Level]
Discussed	Findings discussed by phone with [Ordering Clinician] on [Current Date/Time].

Macro-based management of incidental findings

A variety of incidental findings in general radiologic practice require imaging or clinical follow up. These include incidental pulmonary nodules, thyroid nodules, mediastinal adenopathy, among many more possibilities. Medical societies including the American College of Radiology have published guidelines on how these should be followed. In some cases, these can be complex and difficult to recall during busy shifts. PowerScribe has default functionality that provides guidance on the follow up of incidental findings. However (at time of writing), this feature often requires a dozen or so clicks and other inputs, making it cumbersome to use.

It is possible to handle incidental findings far more efficiently using macros. We developed a set of macros in which all commonly used guidelines can be accessed within 1-2 clicks. The recommendations are built into picklist options for each incidental finding based on imaging characteristics and patient risk factors. Use of nested macro functionality also allows a user to call a directory of all available incidental finding macros ("macro incidental"), and select the relevant finding from a list. These tools are available in the online directory and are one example of how thoughtful macro creation can used for clinical decision support.

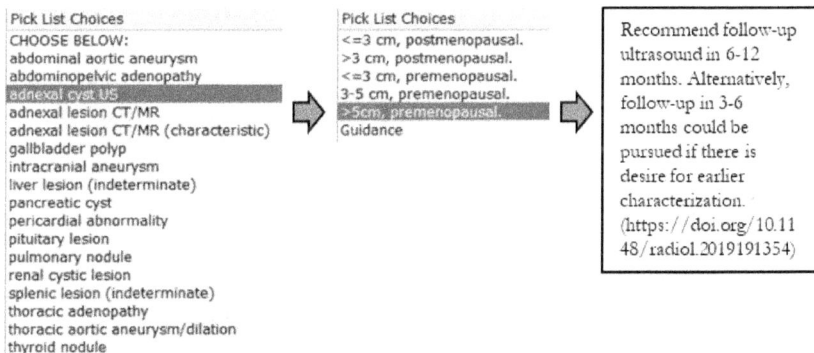

Figure: Example structure and use of a nested macro to guide follow up recommendations for incidental findings.

Reference macros for classification schemes and practical information

Many pathologies seen in radiology have a corresponding classification or grading scheme which can guide clinical management. Many classification schemes are sufficiently complex that they cannot be condensed in a picklist macro. However, creation of simple "reference" (or "info sheet") macros can still aid efficiency in these cases by minimizing the need to open a web browser or look up the same reference again and again. Reference values can be called into a report for easy reference and deleted before the reported is published. The relevant information may alternatively be viewed in the AutoText panel during active dictation.

Reference sheets can also be created to collect important phone numbers, internet links, and other workflow related information that is more practice-specific. Depending on individual and practice needs, making reference material available as systems macros can improve dissemination and accessibility as well as minimize the need to duplicate macros into personal profiles.

Below are examples of reference macros created at our own institution, also available for download from the online repository:

- American Association for the Surgery of Trauma (AAST) injury scoring scales
- Ankle Brachial Index (ABI) interpretation criteria
- Carotid ultrasound stenosis criteria
- Endometrial thickness (normal/abnormal values)
- Early pregnancy failure criteria
- Pancreatic duct size (normal/abnormal values)
- PIOPED II criteria
- Renal artery stenosis criteria
- Sutures and fontanels (normal/abnormal fusion timelines)
- Thyroid size (normal/abnormal values)
- Tibial plateau fracture classification (Schatzker)
- Transcranial Doppler vasospasm criteria

Reference materials which may be more institution specific include PACS/workflow tips for post-processing specific MRI exams, processing of coronary calcium scores, and guides to protocolling studies. Any number of differing resources may be made efficiently accessible within PowerScribe, providing easy access during clinical work.

Optimizing default templates

A few general principles can help improve the efficiency of default templates. Each will provide a small improvement. Together, these small efficiencies added up to noticeably faster reporting.

- Create default templates for each technique, protocol, or clinical scenario.
  - o Default templates which pre-populate the correct technique and other required information can be an efficient way to ensure compliance with billing requirements.
  - o Many institutions will have an existing library of such templates. The next step is often to make sure there is complete coverage of all possible exam orders and assign system (or personal) templates.
  - o It is prudent to create distinct templates for studies as similar as "CT abdomen pelvis with contrast," "CT abdomen pelvis without contrast," and "CT abdomen pelvis with and without contrast" to preempt future requests for billing-related corrections. In other cases, such as for pelvic ultrasounds, subtle differences in technique may be resolved with a technique picklist.
- Note that the format of macros plays a large role in report readability and ease of editing.
  - o Consider using bullet points (separate lines) for findings in templates, rather than having them all run together in one paragraph. Structured formatting can make it much easier to find what needs to be modified when dictating.
  - o Consider putting a space between each series of bullet points corresponding to a large anatomic compartment such as between the chest and abdomen-pelvis on a "pan-scan." This can make it even easier to find what needs to be edited in active dictation.

- o Consider adding formatting such as bold, underline, italics, and all-caps to portions of report text (e.g., headings and field names in structured reports) to assist in the visual navigation of templates during reporting. Depending on the specifics of EHR integration, some of this formatting may be retained in the report available to clinical staff, improving readability for multiple users.
- o Organized templates make it easier for clinicians and other radiologists to read a report. It also makes it easier to find what one is looking for when reading follow ups for one's own studies.
- Consider having only one anatomic site or pertinent negative per dictation ("Fill-in") field, even within structured reports.
  - o For example, instead of "No fracture or dislocation," have "No fracture." as one field and "No dislocation." as the next. This way, if there is a fracture but no dislocation, you need only dictate over the first field, without modifying or re-dictating the other.
  - o Similarly, "No acute intracranial hemorrhage or ischemic infarct," could be written instead as "No acute intracranial hemorrhage" and "No evidence of ischemic infarct." Numerous other potential findings could be formatted this way for easier editing.
  - o Having only one finding per dictation field also makes it easier to locate where in the template you need to click or tab to make changes.
- Use picklists within templates as much as possible to minimize the need for dictation.
  - o Any time there are a small number of common findings for a given field, consider creating a picklist instead of dictating the same phrase every time. The following are a few categories of findings that can shortened into picklists.
    - Differing severities of pulmonary edema on chest radiograph.
    - Differing distributions of airspace opacity or consolidation on chest radiograph.
    - No thrombus/occlusive thrombus/non-occlusive thrombus on DVT studies.

- Differing patterns of paranasal sinus mucosal thickening/secretions on head and neck imaging.
- Differing severities of spinal stenosis on spinal imaging.
   o A picklist with no default value can be used to quickly include a common auxiliary finding. An option called "allow empty" can be used with picklists to avoid PowerScribe pop-ups upon signing reports with Fill-in fields left empty.

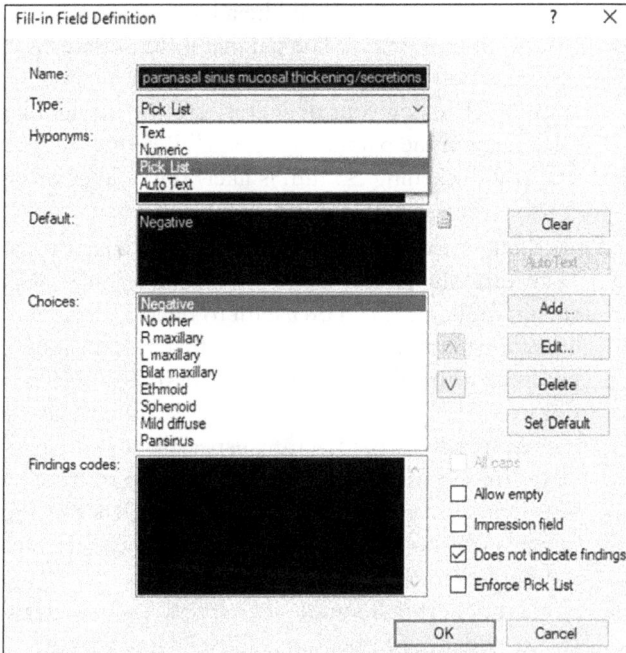

Figure: Creation of a pick list from macro fill-in field options.

- Where appropriate, consider using pertinent negatives as default text rather than blanket terms such as "unremarkable" or "normal." Findings which are technically not normal, but clinically insignificant could then be omitted or added only as desired.
   o For example, instead of "The vasculature is unremarkable," in an abdominal CT template, consider using default wording such as "No aortic aneurysm." The pertinent negative statement allows

one to avoid mentioning vascular calcification, other changes of atherosclerosis, or anatomic variations which are unlikely to impact care, but which can technically contradict sweepingly worded default text. (One's search pattern should still include all potential sites of abnormalities, beyond what is listed in default text.)

o Similarly, "No acute or aggressive osseous lesion" may be preferable to "The osseous structures are unremarkable." Degenerative changes could be added only as relevant.

o Instead of modifying "The paranasal sinuses are clear" every time you see a polyp/mucous retention cyst or minimal secretions, consider changing your default macro to "no significant mucosal thickening in the paranasal sinuses." Research suggests that mucosal thickening ≤3 mm is likely physiologic or of no consequence and does not necessarily warrant mentioning.

• Consider building exam-appropriate caveats into default text.

o Many differing exam types will only have limited sensitivity for certain findings. It can be useful to build a recognition of these limitations into the default text so that modification is not necessary when the limitation is of particular relevance.

o For example, single view radiographs of the pelvis will have limited sensitivity for fracture, especially in older patients. It may be technically incorrect to say "there is no fracture" when sensitivity is expected to be low. "No evidence of fracture" remains true no matter the limitations of a study, and may be a more efficient choice of default text.

o Similarly, chest radiograph default text might better say that there is "no evidence of pneumonia" (or "consolidation") given at best moderate sensitivity for these abnormalities.

o Head CTs often do not include the entirely of the orbits (or paranasal sinuses). Default statements like "no orbital pathology" might best be replaced with statements such as "no evidence of acute orbital pathology" or "no acute orbital pathology seen."

o Particularly when the clinical question is directed at potential findings for which an exam has limited sensitivity, appropriately couched default text (which requires no additional marginal effort for each dictation), reduces the need to edit the template to more specifically account for these limitations.

Pick List Choices	No significant paranasal sinus mucosal thickening/secretions seen.]
Negative	No significant mastoid effusion seen.]
No other	No acute or aggressive osseous lesions identified]
R maxillary	
L maxillary	IMPRESSION:
Bilat maxillary	No evidence of acute intracranial abnormality]
Ethmoid	
Sphenoid	YNHH Radiology Notify System Classification: [Routine]
Mild diffuse	
Pansinus	

Pick List Choices	Polypoid mucosal thickening/secretions in the right maxillary sinus.
Negative	No other significant paranasal sinus mucosal thickening/secretions.
No other	No significant mastoid effusion seen.]
R maxillary	No acute or aggressive osseous lesions identified]
L maxillary	
Bilat maxillary	IMPRESSION:
Ethmoid	No evidence of acute intracranial abnormality]
Sphenoid	
Mild diffuse	YNHH Radiology Notify System Classification: [Routine]
Pansinus	

Figure: Use of pertinent negatives, picklist options (top panel for normal; bottom panel for right maxillary sinus mucosal thickening), and implied caveats for description of findings at the paranasal sinuses and other sites.

- Consider voice navigation of reports
  - Many radiologists will tab through dictation fields in a template using Dictaphone buttons or by clicking into the report. Another way of navigating the template involves calling the name of individual fields to jump directly to fields in PowerScribe by saying "Field [field name]." If the "talking fields" option is enabled, the field label will be read back as confirmation. Using this function, it is possible to dictate without looking away from the study. Short or intuitive naming of templates facilitates this work style.
  - Intuitive names for pick list options work similarly. With the dictation cursor on the picklist field in Powerscibe, one need only say the name (or just first set of unique syllables) of the picklist option to select it. It is best to avoid common words as picklist labels, to avoid accidental selection with free dictation. Alternatively, one can also select pick list options numerically. For example, the second option can be selected by dictating "pick two."

o Another means of speeding up dictation includes the use of "findings mode" in PowerScribe. Such a dictation mode allows a radiologist to free-dictate findings, which are then re-organized into the specific fields of a structured report based on keywords within the free dictation text. However, this is highly dependent on precise template architecture (see hyponyms and "does not indicate findings" option in Fill-in fields). Findings mode is therefore uncommonly used and may only be advantageous in niche scenarios.

o Note that it is possible to alter the insertion site of an active dictation by clicking at a new location before finishing dictating. Strategic slowing of speech can grant an extra second to find the appropriate field. This function can help correct errors in dictation navigation on-the-fly whether using voice or visual navigation of reports.

o Generally, visual navigation of reports is sufficiently fast for most radiologists. There are many approaches to efficient reporting however, and voice navigation can be advantageous for some.

Nesting AutoTexts and modules

AutoTexts can be nested into one another: when editing a Fill-in field, select the AutoText option from the "type" drop-down menu. AutoTexts can also be nested as options in picklists. This may be useful for common findings that require further clarification or grading, such as the severity of spinal stenosis. Nested macro functionality can be a means of building inherent logic into templates, which facilitates both education and decision support.

Use of nested AutoTexts can also be used for efficient management of templates that share components. For example, a module like "header" including universal Merge field information can be the start of every template. A module like "findings CT head" can be included as part of templates for CT head, CT head with contrast, CTA head, CTA head and neck, and more. Such AutoTexts can be characterized as "modules," which prevents inadvertent insertion by name during active dictation. Though there is greater startup cost for such a paradigm, it enables easier long-term maintenance of AutoText libraries. A change in one module flows through to every template that contains it.

One should be wary that nested AutoText links are broken when cloned between users or when modules are renamed. If standalone portability is a high priority, module text could be manually pasted into templates to remove dependencies. Linking can also be restored manually after cloning or renaming.

Differing situational default templates

Fundamentally, each exam code can only be assigned one default AutoText per context. This can be subdivided by age (say, for unique pediatric templates), gender, or patient status (outpatient versus inpatient). Conversely, an AutoText can be assigned to one or multiple exam codes and then flagged as the default; look for the right-pointing arrow icon when the "Fields" panel is selected.

Sometimes a single type of exam is best reported using differing templates based on the clinical scenario or indication. For example, CT exams for planning of sinus surgery will likely require a differing approach than CT exams for complications of acute sinusitis. Differing protocols, such as brain MRIs performed differently for stroke evaluation, epilepsy, or CSF leak may all be associated with the same imaging code, but best dictated using differing templates. Similarly, right upper quadrant ultrasounds, pediatric appendix ultrasounds, sonographic ascites surveys, and any other incomplete abdominal ultrasound may all share an exam code.

When multiple distinct templates are associated with a single exam code (though not necessarily set as default), they can be organized in several ways:

- Distinct exam codes can be created and mapped to different templates. For example, in the emergency setting, a noncontrast abdomen and pelvis CTs done in prone positioning for flank pain can be assigned a unique exam code.

- The most commonly used report can be set as default. The rest can be selected from a drop-down menu from the "Fields" tab. This requires that the AutoTexts be categorized as "Templates," since "Macro" and "Module" types will not be displayed.

- A separate "parent" template can be created, one consisting of a single picklist which has the various other templates nested as the picklist options. Note that this paradigm introduces a "hard stop" to the workflow, and the benefits must be weighed against the extra required navigation for every case.

Technique	Choose the appropriate technique.
Pick List Choices	
TECHNIQUE:	
Transpelvic W pulsed	
Transpelvic WO pulsed	
Transvaginal transpelvic W pulsed	
Transvaginal transpelvic WO pulsed	
Transvaginal W pulsed	
Transvaginal WO pulsed	

Figure: Example parent template used to prompt selection of appropriate exam technique. Selection from the pick list produces the full reporting template for the associated ultrasound exam.

Common abnormal whole templates

Picklist approaches may be used to populate whole templates for common pathologies or postsurgical changes. Selection of whole reports can remove the need to dictate differing degrees of pulmonary edema, basilar scarring/atelectasis, pneumonia, or facilitate reporting of studies with support devices on chest radiographs. A similar approach can be used for head CTs performed in differing scenarios (stroke code or non-stroke code) as well as common patterns of abnormality. The ultimate utility of such approaches is likely to depend on the case mix at any given practice.

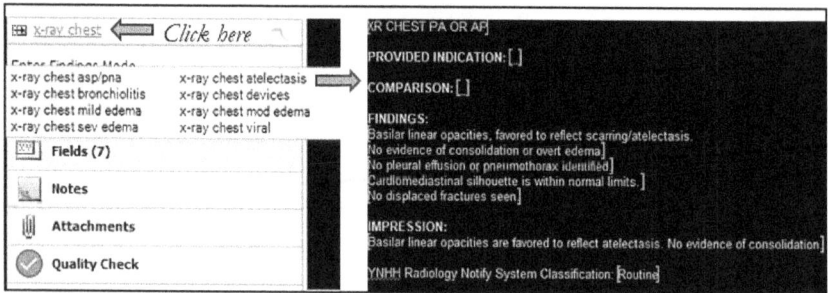

Figure: Example use of template drop-down menu to populate common whole abnormal templates for chest radiographs.

Selected references

- Rak KM, Newell 2nd JD, Yakes WF, Damiano MA, Luethke JM. Paranasal sinuses on MR images of the brain: significance of mucosal thickening. AJR. American journal of roentgenology. 1991 Feb;156(2):381-4.

- McGrath AL, Dodelzon K, Awan OA, Said N, Bhargava P. Optimizing radiologist productivity and efficiency: Work smarter, not harder. European Journal of Radiology. 2022 Oct 1;155:110131.

- Hall FM. The radiology report of the future. Radiology. 2009 May;251(2):313-6.

- Langlotz CP. The Radiology Report: A Guide to Thoughtful Communication for Radiologists and Other Medical Professionals. CreateSpace Independent Publishing Platform. 2015. ISBN: 978-1515174080.

Macro Organization and Special Functions

Long H. Tu

E. Brooke Schrickel

Peter Hung

Introduction

Building well-constructed individual macros provides many improvements in reporting efficiency. In special circumstances, niche functions for organizing, calling, and transferring macros can produce further advances. In this chapter we also review functions that can assist with broader practice management of macro libraries.

Macro shortcuts

Macros in PowerScribe can be called verbally or by using a typed macro shortcut. Most users will be familiar with calling macros using voice command. However, an AutoText can be associated with a "Shortcut" (displayed directly below AutoText name) composed of a string of characters using the AutoText editor. Typing this string into a dictation window followed by the enter key populates the macro without requiring a voice command. This function is most useful when on the phone, when your voice and a hand are diverted. The functionality is potentially further empowered when paired with actions programmed to peripheral devices or using an automation tool like AutoHotKey. Macros can then be added to reports with a single keystroke rather than voice command. This function opens the door for deeper automation of reporting, which is explored in a later chapter.

Figure: AutoText manager panel where macro shortcuts can be created. This chest radiograph macro is then callable by typing "xrc" followed by enter into an active dictation.

Macro folders

For users with large collections of macros, including a variety of exam templates, info sheets, and modules, it can be useful to organize macros into folders. Macros can be added to more than one folder in PowerScribe ("labels" might be a useful way to think about). Folders may be named in such a way that when sorting by folder name during active dictation, the most commonly referenced info sheets populate at the top of the AutoText panel, allowing easy reference. Organization of large macro collections also facilitates updating, export, and sharing.

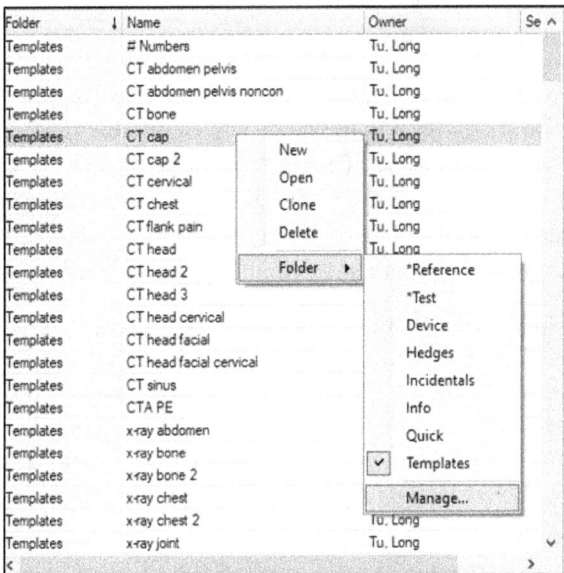

Folder	↓ Name	Owner	Se
Templates	# Numbers	Tu. Long	
Templates	CT abdomen pelvis	Tu. Long	
Templates	CT abdomen pelvis noncon	Tu. Long	
Templates	CT bone	Tu. Long	
Templates	CT cap	Tu. Long	
Templates	CT cap 2	Tu. Long	
Templates	CT cervical	Tu. Long	
Templates	CT chest	Tu. Long	
Templates	CT flank pain	Tu. Long	
Templates	CT head	Tu. Long	
Templates	CT head 2		
Templates	CT head 3		
Templates	CT head cervical		
Templates	CT head facial		
Templates	CT head facial cervical		
Templates	CT sinus		
Templates	CTA PE		
Templates	x-ray abdomen		
Templates	x-ray bone		
Templates	x-ray bone 2		
Templates	x-ray chest		
Templates	x-ray chest 2	Tu. Long	
Templates	x-ray joint	Tu. Long	

Context menu options: New, Open, Clone, Delete, Folder ▶ (*Reference, *Test, Device, Hedges, Incidentals, Info, Quick, ✓ Templates, Manage...)

Figure: Macros can be added or moved between folders from the AutoText editor or from the AutoText panel during active dictation. Folders can be created by selecting "Manage…" from the folder sub-menu.

Systems macros and administrative access

Most practices will have default templates associated with common exams. However, further development of "systems" macros in PowerScribe can improve the dissemination of efficiency-oriented macros to all radiologists within a practice. Systems macros are callable by users whether or not they are cloned into a personal profile.

A collection of basic efficiency macros (using vetted language and formatting) could be shared with new trainees to assist with onboarding. Macros for incidental findings, info sheets, and practice-specific workflows are also high value targets for system macro creation. Systems macros can be organized into sections and placeholder "sections" created for specific collections of macros applicable to many users.

System macros are managed by users with administrative access to PowerScribe. It can be useful to designate a select number of radiologists for administrative access alongside IT managers. Input and feedback from others within the same practice can ensure that the needs of the larger group are met with macro edits. Centralized macro refinement can reduce redundant efforts at personal macro development and promote consensus reporting practices.

Major responsibilities for PowerScribe administration-level users might include:

- Creation and assignment of default templates for all exam types. Priority should be given to the most common exams, though eventually having default templates for all exam codes can be useful.
- Assignment of default templates for new exam codes resulting from advances in scanning capability or modification of image exam coding.
- Updating of macros for greater efficiency, such as with formatting changes, addition of picklists, and integration of custom fields.
- Updating of systems info-sheets and macros whose contents are tied to changes in the radiology literature, such as recommendations for incidental findings.
- Deletion of defunct, unused, or obsolete macros.

- Bulk back-up, import, export, and transfer of macros for individuals and as needed for the practice as a whole.
- Creation of educational or onboarding materials assisting users with macro functionality where relevant.

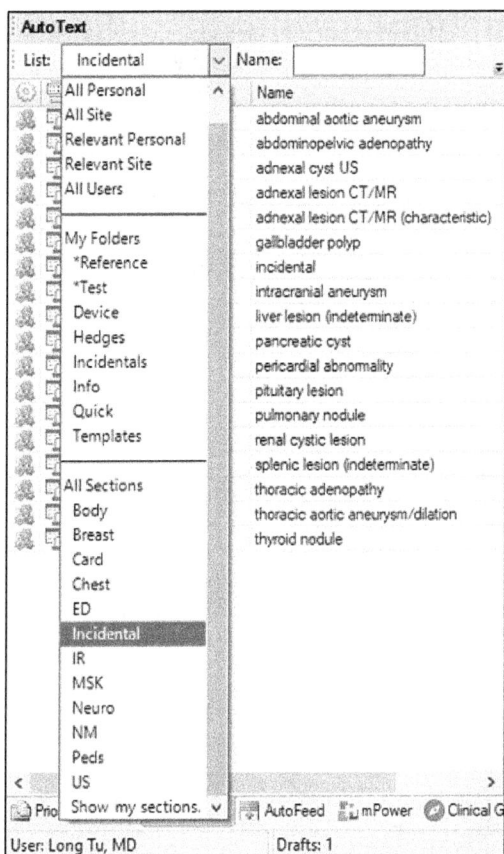

Figure: Systems macros can be viewed during active dictation from a drop-down menu in the AutoText panel. Categories of systems macros can be created for differing subspecialties or for general reporting use.

Macro import, export, and transfer

While whole PowerScribe profiles can be exported as XML files by PowerScribe administrators, many practices may not be willing to import these at a new site or job. Exam code associations and custom field functions are specific to each practice. Individual macros can be exported/saved as RTF files which retain dictations fields and other functionality. This format is far more portable and does not require administrative access to use.

- To save/export a macro:
    - Open the macro from the AutoText Editor.
    - Click File (top left dropdown menu.)
    - Click "Save As…"
    - Save as an RTF file at the desired location.

- To import a saved macro:
    - Click File (top left dropdown menu)
    - Select "Open File…"
    - Select an RTF file from any computer location.
    - Edit as needed.
    - Save to profile.

It is also possible to click and drag RTF files directly into the AutoText Editor textbox or even an active dictation. The RTF format allows the sharing of PowerScribe macros between sites and practices. Import, export, and whole profile transfers can be facilitated using AutoHotKey scripts (a free automation program), which we cover in a later chapter.

Online resources

An online repository of macros can be found at:

- tinyurl.com/fast-rad-macros

The repository has templates for common radiographic, ultrasound, and CT studies. Select MRI exams are also included. Essentially all templates follow the principles outlined in the preceding chapters, with structured formatting, one finding per dictation field, and common findings available as picklists for as many fields as possible.

A selection of efficiency-oriented macros for general radiology is also included. The repository includes "reference" (info sheet) macros, picklist-style macros for incidental findings, and commonly used "hedges."

Custom fields are expected to be institution-specific. Automated import of contrast dose, automated comparison date input, and integrated communication acuity fields will not transfer to other institutions, but may serve as stand-ins if such functions are planned.

Wording and stylistic choices are radiologist-specific and would likely need to be modified to suit specific practice and personal needs. Any macros referencing published guidelines would need to be updated with changes in the relevant literature.

Educational Preparation
(For Residents and Fellows)

Long H. Tu

Kevin Wu

Mahan Mathur

Introduction

Knowing how to learn, what to focus on, and what resources to seek out during training can impact long-term practice efficiency. Having a sense of the demands of independent practice can help trainees track their progress in developing work efficiency.

Structured learning

Education during residency does not necessarily present information in a form that is relevant to clinical practice. Textbooks and lectures often cover pathologies one by one, grouped by organ system or pathologic classification. For example, a single lecture may address brain tumors, intracranial infection, or demyelinating diseases. For each entity, a collection of information is reviewed, including clinical features, imaging appearance, and management options. In practice, it is more useful to organize etiologies by imaging appearance and differential diagnosis. For example, it is useful to know the differential diagnosis for ring enhancing lesions, extra-axial enhancing lesions, or multi-lobar brain lesion. Clinically-oriented education should focus primarily on learning the differential diagnoses for specific imaging appearances and what features differentiate entities within each differential.

It is useful for residents and fellows to re-organize information or direct self-study in way that prepares them for clinical practice. A structured approach to organizing radiologic knowledge can also help identify gaps in understanding and improve recall.

A useful model for how memory may be efficiently stored is called the "method of loci" or popularly "memory palace." Such an approach has been thoroughly described in the literature on learning and is used by those who compete in memory competitions. Briefly, for every exam, radiologists have a search pattern that "visits" every anatomical site. At each site, there is a collection of abnormal findings that might be detected. For each pattern of abnormality, there is differential diagnosis (list of potential etiologies). Each entity is associated with practical knowledge, including distinguishing factors and potential impact on care.

Knowledge obtained during training should be organized into a "journey" guided by one's search pattern, with forks in the road for each finding, and additional paths for each item in a differential diagnosis. At the end of each path is an understanding of how our observations impact patient care. Structuring education this way can facilitate knowing "what to look for" during clinical practice. Having differentials and distinguishing features in mind for any given finding allows rapid interpretation, rather than requiring active recall of individual etiologies. Knowing what imaging features impact management allows focused description and minimizes the reporting of irrelevant detail.

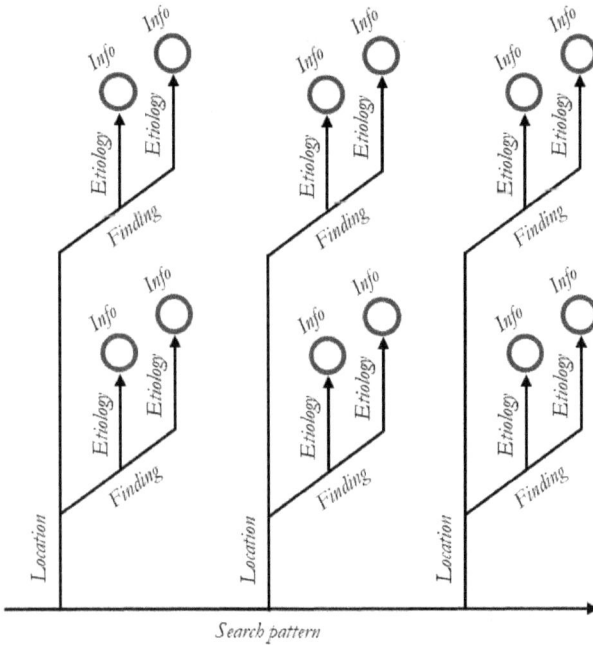

Figure: Conceptual diagram of how information can be logically organized for retrieval during clinical practice. Efficient radiologists have thorough maps of knowledge regarding what findings can be seen at each location, what differential possibilities are associated with each finding, and critical information for major and common pathologies.

A series of questions can aid the organization of radiologic knowledge into this branching tree structure. Anytime a new entity is encountered in clinical practice or independent study, consider:

- On what type of exam(s) is this pathology encountered?
- Where in a search pattern would this be seen?
- What findings would have a differential diagnosis including this entity?
- What features (if any) help distinguish this entity from others in the differential?
- What features or associated findings impact management?

Radiologists who do not naturally or intentionally organize their knowledge can struggle with efficiency. During training, residents may develop sound "book knowledge," yet be predisposed to waffle or hesitate excessively on clinical service. Upon encountering a finding, it can be mentally taxing to sort through one's memory for entities with matching imaging appearances. It is much easier to have differential diagnoses and distinguishing features at the ready. Leveraging prepared knowledge is better and faster.

Benchmarking and feedback

In residency and fellowship programs, it is useful to provide trainees a sense of whether their practical skills and efficiency are progressing. Case volumes for each rotation or even on a day-to-day basis can be extracted and compared with historical ranges or peer summary statistics. Radiology case search applications such as Montage/mPower can assist with this task for those institutions with access. PowerScribe administrators may also extract reports in bulk and provide descriptive statistics. Trainees themselves may assess their own reading volumes and turnaround times compared to peers using the capability in PowerScribe to query reports over arbitrary time scales.

As there are obviously many factors that influence case volumes, such data may only be useful to identify major trends and outliers. We have seen variation in case volumes greater than 200% in training cohorts. Program-specific norms can provide useful guidance to trainees and educators seeking to track progress. Wide variation can indicate the need for personal or program-level efforts to support the development of practical skills.

It should be noted that while the ACGME provides minimum case requirements for graduation from residency (and certain fellowships), these represent a very low threshold. Meeting ACGME case requirements is best considered necessary but not sufficient preparation for independent practice.

Case Log Categories and Required Minimum Numbers
Review Committee for Radiology

Aggregate Logged Imaging Studies

Case Log Categories	Required Minimum Number	CPT Codes
Chest X-ray	1,900	71045, 71046, 71047, 71048
CT Abd/Pel	600	72192, 72193, 72194, 74150, 74160, 74170, 74176, 74177, 74178
CTA/MRA	100	70496, 70498, 70544, 70545, 70546, 70547, 70548, 70549, 71275, 71555, 72159, 72191, 72198, 73206, 73225, 73725, 73706, 74174, 74175, 74185
Mammography	300	77061, 77062, 77065, 77066, 77067
MRI Body	20	71550, 71551, 71552, 72195, 72196, 72197, 74181, 74182, 74183, 74712, 74713
MRI Brain	110	70551, 70552, 70553
MRI Lower Extremity Joints	20	73721, 73722, 73723
MRI Spine	60	72141, 72142, 72146, 72147, 72148, 72149, 72156, 72157, 72158,
PET	30	78459, 78491, 78492, 78608, 78609, 78811, 78812, 78813, 78814, 78815, 78816
US Abd/Pel	350	76700, 76705, 76706, 76770, 76775, 76830, 76856, 76857

Individually Logged Procedures by Residents

Case Log Categories	Required Minimum Number	CPT Codes
Image Guided Bx/Drainage	25	20604, 20606, 20611, 32555, 32557, 49083, 49405, 49406, 49407, 77012, 76942, 77002, 77021

Figure: Minimum case volumes for completion of a US diagnostic residency in 2023. These figures are far lower than what is typically necessary for adequate skill development.

Productivity expectations

Preparing for independent practice is a priority for more senior trainees. Having a sense of volume expectations for attendings, even earlier in training, can inform the development of practical skills. In the U.S., physician services are quantified in RVUs (Relative Value Units) for the purposes of reimbursement. In this chapter, unless otherwise specified, we are referring to "work RVUs," which is the portion of total billed services used to determine radiologist compensation. Practicing radiologists typically read 10,000–15,000 RVUs per year (as estimated in 2019). Private practice radiologists tend to fall on the higher end of this range, with academic radiologists generally on the lower end. There is likely to be variation based on subspecialty, practice specifics, experience, and radiologist preference.

CR/ BMD	
X RAY FOOT 3 VIEWS	0.17
X RAY ABDOMEN AP VIEW (KUB)	0.18
X RAY CHEST SINGLE VIEW	0.18
X RAY SHOULDER 3 VIEWS	0.18
X RAY KNEE 3 VIEWS	0.18
X RAY CHEST PA AND LATERAL	0.22
X RAY CERVICAL SPINE 2-3 VIEWS	0.22
X RAY LUMBAR SPINE 2-3 VIEWS	0.22
X RAY ABDOMEN 2 VIEWS	0.23
BONE MINERAL DENSITY (DEXA)	0.30

US	
US DUPLEX EXT VEINS UNILATERAL	0.45
US NECK SOFT TISSUES	0.56
US ABDOMEN LIMITED	0.59
US KIDNEY COMPLETE	0.74
US ABDOMEN COMPLETE	0.81
US PREGNANCY	0.99
US TRANSVAGINAL with DOPPLER	1.85
US OB DETAILED FETUS (suspected fetal problem)	1.90

Breast Imaging	
US BREAST UNILATERAL	0.73
MAMMOGRAM DIGITAL SCREENING BILATERAL	0.76
MAMMOGRAM DIAGNOSTIC DIGITAL UNILATERAL	0.81
MAMMOGRAM DIAGNOSTIC DIGITAL BILATERAL	1.00
MAMMOGRAM SCREENING 3D TOMOSYNTHESIS BIL.	1.36
MRI BREAST BILATERAL W AND WO CONTRAST	2.39

CT	
CT HEAD WO CONTRAST	0.85
CT SINUS WO CONTRAST	0.85
CT SPINE CERVICAL WO CONTRAST	1.00
CT SPINE LUMBAR WO CONTRAST	1.00
CT SPINE LUMBAR WO CONTRAST	1.00
CT CHEST WO CONTRAST	1.08
CT NECK SOFT TISSUE WITH CONTRAST	1.38
CT RENAL STONE	1.74
CT ABDOMEN PELVIS W CONTRAST	1.82
CTA CHEST (PE) ANGIOGRAPHY	1.82
CT CHEST ABDOMEN PELVIS W CONTRAST	2.98
CTA HEAD AND NECK W AND WO CONTRAST	3.50
CTA TAVR	3.95

MRI	
MRA HEAD WO CONTRAST	1.20
MRI KNEE WO CONTRAST RIGHT	1.35
MRI SHOULDER WO CONTRAST RIGHT	1.35
MRI BRAIN WO CONTRAST	1.48
MRI CERVICAL SPINE WO CONTRAST	1.48
MRI LUMBAR SPINE WO CONTRAST	1.48
MRI ABDOMEN W AND WO CONTRAST	2.20
MRI LUMBAR SPINE W AND WO CONTRAST	2.29
MRI BRAIN W AND WO CONTRAST	2.29
MRI CARDIAC W AND WO CONTRAST	2.60
MRI ABDOMEN AND PELVIS (e.g. ENTEROGRA	4.40
MRI BRAIN AND MRA HEAD/NECK	4.09
MRI TOTAL SPINE W AND WO CONTRAST	6.87

Tables: RVU values for common studies (2023).

To understand how RVU figures translate into daily workload, it can useful to have a sense of the RVU weighting for differing exam types. Generally radiographic studies are 0.20-0.25 RVU. Ultrasound exams are generally 0.5-

1.0 RVU. CT exams are mostly 1.0-2.0 RVU. MRIs are generally 1.0-3.0 RVU. Another way of conceptualizing this is to look at the relative weighting of differing modalities for a single body part. Using abdominal radiographs as the reference, ultrasound is worth 2-4x the RVU, CT is 10-12x, and MRI is 10-20x (depending on specific technique).

Estimating 260 working days (8 weeks of vacation) for a typical radiologist, we can then convert annuals RVUs to expected daily workload (38-58 RVU per day). If reading only abdomen-pelvis CTs, this would be the equivalent of 25-35 exams per day. Reading 50-70 head CT exams or 30-50 cross sectional studies of intermediate weighting (such as chest CT) produces similar RVUs. Mixed modalities would reduce the number of CT exams for the same totals. For example, 80 chest radiographs and 15-25 chest CTs provides a typical workload. Because RVU expectations depend on many factors, these figures should be taken only as a first approximation. A subset of private practice (and academic) jobs will process far more than these ranges.

Prepare for volume

During residency and fellowship, it can useful to seek out a variety of experiences to prepare for attending practice. Lower volume rotations may be an opportunity to develop one's knowledge base, optimize macros, and seek feedback in readouts. However, trainees preparing for general or acute imaging responsibilities would do well to also seek out high-volume, high-complexity experiences. Elective time later in residency is an ideal time to develop practical skills.

There is evidence from other fields that deliberate practice of skills can advance work efficiency. Subtle changes in approach below the level of conscious control, such as learning to speak faster and more clearly in free dictation, developing muscle memory for common tasks, and mental familiarity with common findings, are facilitated by consciously working at the maximum of one's ability. The ceiling of personal capability can be raised by repeated challenges over time. The latter stages of training are ideal for such experiences, as one still has the safety net of an attending radiologist reviewing cases.

Efficiency metrics

Practices looking to recruit radiologists (especially recent graduates) often have an imperfect means of assessing their readiness to handle the workload. Currently the recruiting process involves review of a CV, references, and an interview process. Prior work or training sites can be informative. While some of this information can be used as a proxy for collegiality, knowledge base, and preparation, none of these datapoints provide direct insight into the ability of a radiologist to handle a specific volume of work.

Hiring radiologists that can handle the workload is a greater priority for practices where there are cross-coverage responsibilities or shared workload. In this setting, a radiologist who struggles with case volumes can detract from the work experience of others, while a highly efficient radiologist will be seen as an asset. Accordingly, some hospitals require job applicants to submit case logs of studies interpreted as proof of experience.

As medical practices become increasingly data-driven and case information can be extracted using widely available tools (e.g., Montage/mPower), productivity metrics may play a larger role in radiologist recruitment. If sufficiently detailed, case data can be used to produce estimates of RVU productivity per day, case turnaround-times, and other proxies for work efficiency. More sophisticated metrics are possible with greater granularity of case data. Case logs and productivity metrics hold potential as means for individual radiologists to communicate readiness for job responsibilities and for practices to seek assurance of clinical productivity.

Efficiency curriculum

To the best of our knowledge, practical skills surrounding work efficiency are not included in the ACGME requirements for diagnostic radiology programs. No related material is meaningfully represented on our board or certifying exams. Programs are not necessarily required to have dedicated lectures, learning materials, or other on-boarding processes related to work efficiency. With ever growing demands for diagnostic imaging and increasing expectations in work volume, this may be an oversight.

Ideally, residencies would provide formal instruction in efficient dictation, PACS use, and workflow organization. Training programs may further benefit from teaching at least introductory concepts in macro development, automation, and use of AI-based applications. Graduates of programs with attention to these topics would be well-prepared for the evolving demands of our field.

Selected references

- Muroff LR, Berlin L. Speed versus interpretation accuracy: current thoughts and literature review. American Journal of Roentgenology. 2019 Sep;213(3):490-2.
- Alexander R, Waite S, Bruno MA, Krupinski EA, Berlin L, Macknik S, Martinez-Conde S. Mandating limits on workload, duty, and speed in radiology. Radiology. 2022 Aug;304(2):274-82.
- Diagnostic Radiology Case Log Categories and Required Minimum Numbers. https://www.acgme.org/globalassets/pfassets/programresources/dr_case_log_categories.pdf. Accessed: 11/15/2023.
- Legge EL, Madan CR, Ng ET, Caplan JB. Building a memory palace in minutes: Equivalent memory performance using virtual versus conventional environments with the Method of Loci. Acta psychologica. 2012 Nov 1;141(3):380-90.

Workflow Organization (For Attendings and Practices)

Long H. Tu

E. Brooke Schrickel

Jason Teitelbaum

Introduction

Efficient radiologic practice also involves thoughtful prioritization of tasks during a clinical shift, organization of radiologists into teams, and (at training programs) strategies for working alongside trainees.

Radiology role differentiation

Radiologists are most efficient at interpreting cases when there is minimal interruption. This becomes increasingly true with studies requiring more time or synthesis of complex findings. It is inefficient for all radiologists, including trainees, to simultaneously handle case volume as well as phone calls, consultations, protocols, and other noninterpretive tasks. Teams of radiologists are best differentiated into roles. Concentrating brief, otherwise interruptive tasks into specific roles improves overall efficiency by minimizing the need for radiologists to "task switch." Consultations, protocols, and shorter interpretative tasks are best grouped together. Radiologists and trainees may rotate through differing roles, to allow varied experience and equity of contribution as warranted.

Support staff

A variety of radiology assistants, technologists, and midlevel practitioners can further improve the efficiency of radiology teams by handling tasks that do not strictly require a physician. Phone calls, contacting referring clinicians, and triaging consultations may be shifted to non-physician staff. Depending on their training, radiology assistants may also help with protocolling and basic procedures. Scribes are less commonly used in radiology than other medical specialties, though may help fill roles in niche scenarios.

Ideally, measurements on ultrasound studies are automatically imported to the dictation software. Where this is not possible, ultrasound technologists can be trained to fill in worksheets and provide diagrams of more complex findings. Scanned worksheets available in the medical record can facilitate reference while dictating. Experienced ultrasound technologists may also be trained to screen for study quality and completeness, to minimize the need for radiologists to engage in interruptive quality assurance activities.

The same principles can be applied to any interpretative service requiring data entry for reports. Assistants may expedite the input of measurements, using worksheets or PACS annotation for TAVR planning and tumor follow-up studies. Supporting roles handling noninterpretive tasks are an opportunity for programs to create internal moonlighting for residents and medical students, who may have familiarity with existing workflows.

Asynchronous and automated communication

In systems where phone calls require frequent redirection, use of a phone tree can provide a buffer to work interruptions. Asynchronous communication with technologists for protocols can allow chunking of potentially interruptive tasks. Text communication integrated with PACS is perhaps most intuitive for these purposes. HIPAA-compliant smart phone text applications can allow noninteractive communication with clinicians. Critical results notification and consultation can be handled with such technology if there is broad implementation in a health system. For procedural services, a text-based paging system can also be less interruptive (and less jarring) than conventional pagers.

Prioritize skill development for high-volume exams

In any setting, there will be a set of studies that dominate the volume of work that is performed. Developing skills or macros to become as efficient as possible with the most common exams will pay the greatest dividends in overall work speed. In general and emergency radiology, radiographs are often the highest volume modality, with chest radiographs the most common exam. Among all CTs, head and cervical CTs can represent the majority of volume. The fastest emergency radiologists are often particularly efficient at reporting radiographs and head-cervical CTs. As another example, the most efficient neuroradiologists often have highly developed strategies and macros for brain MRIs and head and neck CTAs as well as for detailing degenerative change on spinal MRI. Similar principles will apply with high volume exams in other subspecialties. At the practice level, dissemination of tools to assist with high-volume exams would be expected to have the greatest impact among efficiency-oriented quality improvements.

Case acuity mix and timestamp organization

Differing practice settings may require interpretation of differing mixes of urgent and non-urgent cases. Mix of case acuity, shift organization, and concurrent responsibilities related to non-clinical responsibilities all impact the efficiency of a practice.

In the scenario where cases are primarily of urgent nature and organized by "timestamp," irregular groupings of case volume over the course of a shift may produce inefficient use of radiologist time. There may be lulls during shifts where radiologists are awaiting studies to interpret. A sudden increase in volume near the end of shifts can keep physicians on shift longer than usual, at times where mental fatigue and a sense of urgency to finish work makes error most likely. For practice settings with a "timestamp" organization and high case acuity, the introduction of overlapping or swing shifts can help smooth the effects of exam "boluses" and mitigate irregularities in case volume. As needed cross-coverage between physical sites can also smooth volume irregularities. Shared work responsibilities require a team-oriented culture and associated policies. If swing shifts are utilized, several radiologists will likely be utilizing the same reading lists; communication methods must be established to prevent group inefficiencies as a result of a single exam being previewed by more than one radiologist.

At our institution, acute imaging shifts with overlapping swing shifts have greater control of case volume. Shifts without a backup mechanism to handle spikes in volume are associated with wider variations in total work time and have greater risk for delays in care. Lack of control in shift duration and volume is a contributor to burnout and professional dissatisfaction.

More flexibility in work organization occurs when handling primarily outpatient or non-emergent imaging. Radiologists may work whenever and at whatever pace they prefer. Similar principles of cross-coverage and overlapping or staggered shifts may still apply if the organization of responsibilities allows spikes in volume. Due to greater flexibility, shifts composed entirely of non-emergent cases may be the best match for remote work. The efficiency improvements related to self-directed pacing may also allow handling of higher case volumes on a per-shift basis.

Inefficiencies related to unpredictable case volumes can also be mitigated whenever possible through organizing shifts with a variety of case acuity. A radiologist whose responsibilities includes a mix of non-emergent, urgent, and acute/life-threatening cases can work more continuously than one whose responsibilities include only acute responsibilities. Cases may be prioritized based on acuity and non-emergent volume may be handled when there is a lull in emergent cases. Mixed acuity shifts can produce a balance in timeliness of care and efficient staff allocation.

At our institution, a small proportion of shifts carry such cases mixes. These shifts are generally associated with the greatest efficiency in use of radiologist time. Ideally, improvements in shift design can save time for individual radiologists and maximize clinical productivity per hour of work.

As an important caveat, in practice settings where radiologists attend to a variety of non-clinical responsibilities, lulls in clinical volume do not necessarily produce inefficiency. Radiologists at academic institutions may use gaps in clinical demand for teaching, brief research tasks, or administrative work. Any radiologist could make use of lower clinical demand for breaks, directed reading, or efficiency-oriented activities like macro development. Still, repeated task switching can inhibit overall productivity.

Notably, many other healthcare systems face similar challenges with optimizing operations and queuing networks; randomness ensures there will always be peaks and troughs of volume. However, administrators need to analyze data and search for seasonality to create the best staffed practices where radiologist supply matches clinical demand. Thoughtful shift design and staffing practice can yield positive impacts on radiologist efficiency and work satisfaction.

Considerations for attendings working with trainees

At academic institutions, radiologists may supervise and work alongside trainees. Specific workflow practices can improve both clinical productivity and the value of teaching in academic settings. Consider the following tips for working with trainees.

- Maintain skills for reading cases independent of trainees.
  - o There are many circumstances where dictating cases without trainees improves efficiency. Radiologists employed for long periods at academic programs are at risk for atrophy of practical skills related to PACS navigation and reporting. Attendings who depend on trainees to dictate cases can suffer stress related to lower self-efficacy and may be susceptible to bias from preliminary trainee reports. Dependence on trainee labor can also be disadvantageous to control of workhours. Maintained practical skills can be leveraged to produce free time on service, which can then be invested in teaching, research, and other pursuits.
- In acute and urgent settings, preview cases as soon as possible.
  - o In many PACS and workflow orchestrators, it is possible to preview images as an exam begins, before designation as "complete" by technologists. In acute and urgent settings, previewing exams allows one to triage cases based on a preliminary assessment of case complexity and acuity. Previewing cases can also involve looking at prior studies, prior reports, and reviewing the medical record.
  - o It can also be advantageous to begin dictating studies prior to their completion, as in some cases, there will be enough images to begin analyzing findings. For example, having only thin section CT images is sufficient to report on the whole study, as all other reconstructions and slice thicknesses can be produced in MPR viewers. If starting reports on incomplete studies, remember to hold the final report until the study is formally completed or otherwise check that unexpected images were not subsequently added by the technologists.

o   Previewing high acuity cases can make a direct impact on patient care for cases where timeliness strongly impacts outcomes (e.g., stroke, sepsis, and limb ischemia). Triaging and drafting reports as soon as possible for all studies can help mitigate sharp spikes in case volume when they occur.

o   It can be useful to handle simple or negative cases without a trainee. Cases may be triaged to attending-only reporting based on preview of images or pre-test probability of complexity based on patient demographics, study indication, and clinical scenario. Residents, especially early in training, may not have a sense as to what findings are important to convey. Editing lengthy though ultimately "negative" or "stable" reports can be slower than handling such cases independently.

o   It can be useful to assign cases with classic or otherwise instructive findings to junior trainees as valuable learning experiences. Similarly, complicated cases could be triaged to more senior trainees. An extra set of eyes from experienced residents or fellows can be helpful for minimizing detection error, satisfaction of search, and other potential cognitive missteps for complex cases. Trainees can aid efficiency on exams requiring extensive measurements and analysis of abnormality. Of course, junior trainees benefit from tackling both straightforward and challenging cases. In general, optimizing the matching of case complexity to trainee ability can yield improvements in workflow, education, and even morale.

• Teach practical skills. Teach early. Teach often.

o   The body of medical and radiologic knowledge that trainees need to acquire during residency and fellowship is too large to pass on in a meaningful way during on-service teaching.

o   However, there are many high-priority practical skills in radiology that are often best learned at the workstation. Such skills include search patterns for the most common studies, commonly used shortcuts within PACS, and means of efficiently navigating the dictation software. Trainees require encouragement to apply knowledge obtained in didactic formats. The earlier key skills can be taught, the more efficient residents and fellows become, and the more helpful they will be in assisting with the clinical workload.

o   In additional to practical topics, engagement with the teaching mission improves the culture at academic practices. Positive experiences can improve trainee enthusiasm and willingness to provide the highest quality care on clinical shifts. Positive experiences in the reading room can assist with later recruitment efforts for academic projects, fellowship positions, and even future faculty. Interactions at the workstation are perhaps the most powerful means at demonstrating the sort of mentorship a trainee can expect, should they join a research group or other academic effort.

- Consider how much report editing is truly necessary.
   o   In training programs, there is a strong correlation between the amount of report editing performed by attending radiologists and their work efficiency. Attendings who edit reports extensively, especially for stylistic choices, are often much slower than those who restrict edits to clinically impactful findings.
   o   It's important to recognize that most clinicians and even radiologists read only the impression section of reports. Technically correct but awkwardly worded text in the body of reports can often be left as is, if there is no expected impact on clinical care.
   o   Most radiologists have personal stylistic preferences. For those with strong preferences, it can be useful to indicate these verbally to trainees (ideally early in a rotation) and to use macros to input commonly used phrases rather than perform repetitive editing. Utilizing macros should especially be encouraged, to prevent egregious dictation errors (e.g., incorrect laterality or unintended absence of a "no"). Providing specific templates to trainees and preemptive education are other valuable strategies to maintain stylistic consistency.

Selected references

- Halsted MJ, Froehle CM. Design, implementation, and assessment of a radiology workflow management system. American Journal of Roentgenology. 2008 Aug;191(2):321-7.
- Do HM, Spear LG, Nikpanah M, Mirmomen SM, Machado LB, Toscano AP, Turkbey B, Bagheri MH, Gulley JL, Folio LR. Augmented radiologist workflow improves report value and saves time: a potential model for implementation of artificial intelligence. Academic radiology. 2020 Jan 1;27(1):96-105.
- Shah SH, Atweh LA, Thompson CA, Carzoo S, Krishnamurthy R, Zumberge NA. Workflow interruptions and effect on study interpretation efficiency. Current Problems in Diagnostic Radiology. 2022 Nov 1;51(6):848-51.

Physiological and
Cognitive Optimization

Long H. Tu

Nadia Solomon

Cicero T. Silva

Introduction

An often-underappreciated factor in practice efficiency is the optimization of the radiologist's physical and mental state. Numerous factors may impact the physiologic and cognitive abilities of a physician, which then impact work efficiency. We will review the most salient and modifiable factors.

Breaks during work

Evidence suggests that breaks in cognitive work are beneficial for performance. While optimal break duration and frequency are likely to vary by person, shift responsibility, and a variety of other factors, breaks of 10-20 minutes taken every 1-2 hours have been associated with greater work productivity. The more draining the cognitive task, the longer duration of break may be required. Physical activity, relaxation techniques, food, and hydration as needed can improve the positive impact of breaks. Well-timed breaks can improve the quality and overall efficiency of the care provided, compared to when no breaks are taken at all.

To resist the pressure to never leave the workstation, it can be useful to develop habits (or personal guidelines) for when breaks are to be taken, such as after a certain number of studies or at specific time intervals. Arranging cross-coverage may be helpful with high acuity case volume. Efficiency-oriented strategies are synergistic – higher work efficiency in any domain can improve the ability to comfortably take breaks and maintain stamina through longer shifts. In some instances, an inability to step away may relate to broader issues with practice organization such as unmanageable volume, which may need be addressed at a systems level. Simply put, work environments and cultures that allow for appropriate breaks are likely to aid long-term efficiency, in addition to perhaps more obvious positive effects on work satisfaction.

Optimize stress for efficiency

It can be useful to recognize that a certain degree of stress or challenge in work can be beneficial to performance. Demands that are beyond one's capability can produce a vicious cycle of worsening stress and declining efficiency. On the other hand, work expectations that are far below one's ability may produce boredom or disengagement. Having "enough" mental stimulation can be particularly important in maintaining alertness on off-hours or overnight work. Calibrated appropriately, challenges can induce a state of "flow," which is experienced as an enjoyable absorption in work that requires one's full attention. The organization of work responsibilities is a major driver of whether radiologists will feel optimally engaged on service. Individuals may be able to alter the degree of subjective challenge by regulating concurrent activities such as socializing, teaching, and administrative tasks as clinical demand fluctuates. If juggling multiple responsibilities, "chunking" of successive tasks requiring full attention is preferred to "multi-tasking" in which rapid switching between tasks can be detrimental to productivity. As always, it is useful to minimize stress from unnecessary distraction, such as through silencing phone notifications and triaging non-clinical tasks to support staff.

Physical activity prior to work

Research suggests that physical activity prior to cognitive work improves performance. Improved cognitive performance is most consistently found after durations of physical activity of at least 20 minutes. Longer durations are associated with greater benefits so long as dehydration and excessive fatigue are avoided. If there will be a delay (i.e., greater than 20 minutes) between the end of exercise and the commencement of cognitive tasks, the activity should be at least moderate in intensity to derive positive cognitive effects. Lighter physical activity is beneficial if cognitive tasks are performed concurrently or immediately after exercise. Underlying physical fitness is a positive modulating factor, increasing the benefit of physical activity on cognitive performance.

Practically speaking, radiologists who exercise routinely outside of work may consider doing so before rather than after clinical work, to benefit from the cognitive effects of acute exercise. Planning physical activity earlier during waking hours can also be beneficial to sleep hygiene and stabilization of circadian rhythms. Obviously, this is not always possible with conventional work hours and while juggling non-work responsibilities. Radiologists working late and evening shifts may have greater flexibility to take advantage of these strategies.

Other approaches to leverage the positive influence of physical activity include taking walking breaks earlier in the day, commuting by biking or walking whenever possible, and even engaging in light physical activity during work.

Light physical activity during work

Sitting for extended periods of time at the workstation is detrimental to long-term health as well as mental function. The negative health impact of working as radiologist is further exacerbated for those who have long commutes by car or other sedentary means of transportation. Inactivity can be associated with loss of quality and length of life comparable to smoking, not to mention long-term effects on cardiovascular and neurovascular health. Both acute and chronic effects of inactivity on cognitive function may compromise work quality and efficiency.

Use of standing desks can be helpful by allowing alternation between standing and sitting. Low level physical activity such as stretching, fidgeting ("non-exercise activity thermogenesis"), and pacing may also help blunt the impact of sedentary work. These are feasible in almost all work settings.

Perhaps the greatest improvement in performance is gained by engaging in physical activity *during* cognitive tasks. The greatest improvements are associated with low or low-moderate intensity aerobic activity such as walking or easy cycling. Higher intensity physical activity, despite being associated with improved performance after the exercise is concluded, is associated with decreased cognitive performance while the exercise is being performed. One study of radiologists using treadmill desks found similar *accuracy* in detection of pulmonary nodules on chest CT whether walking at 1.5 mph or sitting; however, while walking radiologists required 22% *less time* for study interpretation. While this was a small trial, the conclusions are in line with similar findings of improved attention, working memory, problem solving, verbal fluency, and decision making in studies of physical activity outside of radiology. Other research recognizes the ability of physical activity to improve mood and mitigate work stress, even for as long as 24 hours after "exposure" to acute exercise.

A number of radiologists at our institution use under-desk treadmills, ellipticals, and stationary bikes during clinical work. Treadmills with an incline can aid with stability and minimize impact while walking and are the most popular solution. Equipment is available at several sites within our health system and is used in remote offices. Even walking at 0.5-1.5 miles per hour intermittently during a clinical workday can add up to many miles. Those using treadmills consistently usually cover 4-8 miles during a clinical shift. Intermittent users may cover 1-2 miles. Particularly ambitious trainees have reported walking as many as 13 miles during an 8-hour shift. Subjective reports suggest neutral or favorable effects on clinical ability, productivity, and stress management, compatible with existing literature.

Figure: Example devices (from left to right, top to bottom, not to relative scale) include an under-desk treadmill by Bifanuo, another by Egofit, an under-desk elliptical by Niceday, an under-desk bike by Himaly, and a conventional stationary bike by Sunny (that can be rolled under a workstation).

Biking during clinical work provides similar benefits as walking, through may be even easier to manage due to less head motion. Many conventional stationary bikes can be rolled under a desk; specific under-desk products are also available. Modest biking speeds, comparable to cycling outdoors at 10 miles per hour, are sustainable for long durations during clinical shifts. Depending on baseline conditioning, it is possible to bike the equivalent of 40-60 miles during clinical work. Even substantially less physical activity (e.g., a single hour of walking or biking) represents a profound improvement over sitting for the entirety of a clinical shift.

No single physical activity during work will be appealing or possible for all radiologists. It can be useful to trial a variety of approaches. Reading rooms at our institution are also equipped with pull-up bars, resistance bands, grip trainers, and yoga mats. Resistance training has also been found to have positive effects on cognitive function. Stretching is particular useful for stress relief and for prevention of musculoskeletal strain related to prolonged sitting.

Radiologists who sit most of the day or with poor posture are at higher risk for exaggerated kyphosis, excessive shoulder internal rotation, and weakness of core muscles and hip flexors. Back extension, shoulder external rotation, as well as hip extension are movements that could be prioritized for both stretching and strengthening. Attention to these potential imbalances could be helpful in any physical conditioning outside of work. Spinal decompression and traction devices can reduce the strain of prolonged sitting for those with sufficient space in a home office or particularly accommodating work settings.

It should be noted, however, that light aerobic activity has the strongest evidence and largest effect size for improving mental function. Any time engaged in physical activity during work reduces the need for exercise outside of work to maintain general health.

Integrating physical activity with clinical work is among the most powerful tools in improving work satisfaction and efficiency in radiology. We suggest consideration of under-desk treadmills, bikes, and other devices to derive benefit to mental acuity, mood, and long-term health.

Hydration, caffeination, and fueling

One's ability to perform complex cognitive work is also impacted by numerous metabolic factors. The greatest impact on work productivity related to metabolic state likely involves the timing and content of meals. Snacks with low glycemic index and smaller meals may be advantageous for maintaining consist energy during clinical work. It can be useful to avoid large, carbohydrate-rich, or high-sodium meals to minimize the loss of mental acuity that can occur in post-prandial states. Snacks high in simple carbohydrates can also produce insulin spikes and circulatory changes potentially impairing mental acuity. The negative effects of post-prandial states and any sleep deprivation can be mitigated with caffeine intake. The effect of caffeine on individuals is highly variable, requiring calibration for optimal effect.

Some radiologists in our group work primarily in a fasted state, citing subjective improvements in mental clarity. The literature is conflicting, however, regarding the impact of fasting on cognitive performance. Most studies suggest that intermittent fasting or skipping meals has a neutral or adverse effect on cognitive performance; however, there seems to be greater evidence of benefit for long-term cognitive wellbeing. Whether fasted states are beneficial seems likely to vary between individuals and would need to be assessed on a personal basis.

On the other hand, as everyone ultimately requires nourishment, lulls in clinical demand offer efficient times to eat and drink. Moderate snacking during work hours may reduce the need to eat at other times. In later chapters, we discuss ways to maximize the ability to work with a single hand or to automate study navigation which can facilitate snacking during work.

While accomplishing more non-work activities at work is a viable means of improving overall efficiency, it is important to recognize the potential for unintended negative consequences. A work culture which incentivizes taking whole meals while working rather than taking time to sit-down with colleagues can have underappreciated negative physical, mental, and emotional effects. Food options chosen primarily for expediency may not be beneficial for long-term health. It can be worthwhile to consider the balance of these various factors when organizing one's workday.

It is obvious that dehydrated states impair mental functioning. However, absence of frank dehydration does not necessarily coincide with optimal hydration. There is some evidence that tea or coffee used for hydration has greater positive impact than water on cognitive performance. Furthermore, these effects do not seem entirely attributable to caffeine (and may be seen with non-caffeinated versions). Rather, positive cognitive effects may result from factors that are either intrinsic to the beverage (e.g., sensory attributes, other compounds) or of a psychological nature (e.g., expectancy). Ideally, sweetened beverages are avoided due to negative metabolic effects. There is some evidence to suggest that fluid solutions providing electrolyte repletion can positively impact cognitive performance. The effect size is expected to be small compared to other factors discussed in this chapter. The influence on work efficiency might only be meaningful in niche scenarios such as when there is existing deficiency related to sickness, fasting, or recent high volume physical activity.

Light exposure

Numerous other factors may impact physiologic and cognitive readiness for demanding work. Individual variations in circadian rhythm impact optimal hours for work. Seeking out and tailoring work responsibilities to coincide with circadian preferences can improve work efficiency as well as quality of life.

Similarly, while radiologists work in low-light environments to improve detection of abnormalities, the absence of natural light, especially in early waking hours, can be disruptive to mental alertness and psychological wellbeing. Exposure to bright or natural light (for at least 15 minutes) within the first few hours of one's day can cue wakefulness and positively influence work performance. In geographies and times of year with minimal sunlight, strategically timed breaks for natural light exposure or the use of therapeutic light devices may be beneficial.

Selected references

- Johnson CR, Besachio DA, Delonga D, Kuzniewski C, Mudge CS. Effect of Dynamic Workstation Use on Radiologist Detection of Pulmonary Nodules on CT. J Am Coll Radiol. 2019 Apr;16(4 Pt A):451-457. doi: 10.1016/j.jacr.2018.10.017. Epub 2019 Feb 27. PMID: 30826237.

- Chang YK, Labban JD, Gapin JI, Etnier JL. The effects of acute exercise on cognitive performance: a meta-analysis. Brain research. 2012 May 9;1453:87-101.

- Jia H, Zack MM, Gottesman II, Thompson WW. Associations of smoking, physical inactivity, heavy drinking, and obesity with quality-adjusted life expectancy among US adults with depression. Value in health. 2018 Mar 1;21(3):364-71.

- Basso JC, Suzuki WA. The effects of acute exercise on mood, cognition, neurophysiology, and neurochemical pathways: A review. Brain Plasticity. 2017 Jan 1;2(2):127-52.

- Chen H, Tao Y, Li MD, Gu Y, Yang J, Wu Y, Yu D, Yuan C. Temporal patterns of energy intake and cognitive function and its decline: a community-based cohort study in China. Life Metabolism. 2022 Aug 1;1(1):94-7.

- Gupta CC, Centofanti S, Dorrian J, Coates A, Stepien JM, Kennaway D, Wittert G, Heilbronn L, Catcheside P, Noakes M, Coro D. Altering meal timing to improve cognitive performance during simulated nightshifts. Chronobiology international. 2019 Dec 2;36(12):1691-713.

- Hindmarch I, Quinlan PT, Moore KL, Parkin C. The effects of black tea and other beverages on aspects of cognition and psychomotor performance. Psychopharmacology. 1998 Sep;139:230-8.

- Cousins AL, Young HA, Thomas AG, Benton D. The effect of hypo-hydration on mood and cognition is influenced by electrolyte in a drink and its colour: A randomised trial. Nutrients. 2019 Aug 24;11(9):2002.

- Masento NA, Golightly M, Field DT, Butler LT, van Reekum CM. Effects of hydration status on cognitive performance and mood. British Journal of Nutrition. 2014 May;111(10):1841-52.
- Gudden J, Arias Vasquez A, Bloemendaal M. The effects of intermittent fasting on brain and cognitive function. Nutrients. 2021 Sep 10;13(9):3166.
- Siraji MA, Kalavally V, Schaefer A, Haque S. Effects of daytime electric light exposure on human alertness and higher cognitive functions: A systematic review. Frontiers in psychology. 2022 Jan 5;12:765750.

Environmental Optimization

Long H. Tu

Lam Tu

Mehmet E. Adin

Introduction

Practice optimization requires fine tuning of environmental factors that can affect radiologist work. Ergonomic design can prevent repetitive strain injuries and other musculoskeletal disorders. Room layout, temperature, ambient sound, ventilation, and numerous other factors influence both comfort and ease of work. Psychosocial factors impact the effectiveness of individuals and teams of radiologists. We discuss the factors with greatest potential influence on work efficiency.

Workstation ergonomics

Radiologists are at risk for hand and wrist repetitive strain injuries related to long hours of computer-based work. Several general principles can help prevent strain, disability, and the loss of work efficiency that results from discomfort.

As a rule of thumb, the eyes should be level with the center of the monitors when sitting straight (or standing if using a standing desk). Slightly higher relative position of the eyes, though no higher than the top of the monitors, can be preferable for some radiologists. The ideal monitor distance from the radiologist is approximately an arm's length (50-75cm). With a greater number of monitors, arrangement in a slight arc can minimize neck strain or the need to move one's chair when viewing different monitors.

Placement of the mouse, keyboard, Dictaphone and other input devices should be within easy reach. Devices should be accessible with the arms relaxed at one's side and the elbows bent near 90 degrees. Use of a mousepad with wrist support can reduce the risk of repetitive stress injuries. Use of offhand devices, a "hands-free" microphone solution, and other peripherals may also reduce the need for repetitive motion and decrease risk of strain. Minimizing excessive wrist extension, flexion, or deviation can help prevent injury. While holding devices, intermittently changing one's hand position and using differing fingers for clicking, scroll wheels, or scroll balls can help minimize strain. Automation of scrolling and repeated user inputs can provide further protect against injury.

Adjustable height desks, chairs, and computer screens are useful to optimize workstation ergonomics. Standing desks can help mitigate some of this risk by allowing alternating standing and sitting. Chairs ideally provide independently adjustable arm rests, back support, seat tilt, seat height, seat length, and neck support to fit personal preferences. Novel reclining desk and chair devices may help mitigate the strain of sitting in the same position for long periods. Footrests can help reduce stress on back muscles. Cushioned mats can be helpful for those using a standing desk to reduce pressure points on the feet. Use of desk treadmills and other exercise equipment discussed in the previous chapter can also vary the biomechanics of work and reduce the harms of inactivity.

Workspace design

In hospital and office settings, radiologists may share a common reading room. It can be useful to designate specific responsibilities for differing physical areas. Radiology assistants, coordinators, and "consult" radiologists are best positioned near the room entrance. The assistant or coordinator can answer phone calls, assist with protocoling, and direct clinicians requesting consultation. The "consult radiologist" can speak with clinicians, manage shorter studies, and engage in other work that is resilient to interruption. At middle room depth, radiologists and any trainees might engage in discussion of cases, teaching, or other activities protected from interruption. At the deepest section of the room, perhaps beyond sound barriers, radiologists can engage with the highest complexity and volume of cases with the greatest protection from distraction. Individual workstations in this section could use sound-dampening dividers to further reduce background noise. With modern remote capabilities, this section of radiologists could be offsite, potentially further shielding work from interruption.

Temperature and air quality

The most comfortable temperature for sedentary work has been reported to be between 20 and 24 °C (68 – 75 °F), with relative humidity between 40 and 60%. Temperatures on the lower end of this range may help retain mental acuity through activating the sympathetic nervous system. Computer workstations and monitors do not just add heat to a room, they can dry the air. Air humidification (especially if local climate is also particularly dry) can help reduce irritation of the eyes, nose, and throat which can inhibit optimal work.

Air flow and air conditioning can impact clinical productivity. Particulate matter and CO_2 from suboptimal air filtration and ventilation can produce slowing of mental processes and fatigue. Air conditioning, fans, and air filters should be considered for both shared reading rooms and remote offices. Cooling and airflow are especially important in rooms with many workstations or in scenarios where physical activity is integrated with clinical work. These considerations are especially relevant in an era where many radiologists construct home workspaces without the guidance that might be available when planning conventional facilities.

Lighting

Ambient light relative to computer luminance influences eyestrain, fatigue, and performance. Ambient lighting should be indirect and glare-free. Blinds and shades should be used to control outside lighting. A combination of overhead lighting and individual desk lighting can meet most needs. Desk lighting should be dimmable and ideally behind monitors to minimize reflection and glare. Dark walls can help minimize reflected light. Even the color of one's clothing and desk materials may contribute to glare or reflection. Dark colors may again be preferrable.

Noise control

Unwanted background noise may affect concentration and productivity. Dividing panels between workstations can reduce noise in work areas requiring uninterrupted concentration. Acoustic ceiling and carpet, matte wall finishes, and acoustic absorption panels on walls can help control ambient noise. Noisy equipment, such as printers and copiers, could be placed away from the radiology reading areas. The implementation of sound barriers and noise mitigation materials is also applicable to the diverse environments encountered with remote workstations.

Other factors

While unwanted sound can hamper work, music or calming ambient sound can positively impact work experience. Any soundtrack is probably most appropriate for solo work or when there is clear consensus in a shared space. The impact of music on work performance depends on music quality (without lyrics may be preferrable for cognitive work), personal factors (mood/musical taste), and the complexity of tasks at hand (any ambient sound might interfere with highly demanding work).

The presence of disorganized desk spaces and cluttered rooms can impede optimal function and contribute to heightened stress levels. Work surfaces should be clear of unnecessary materials. Wires from peripheral devices, monitors, and CPUs can be consolidated using ties, boxes, and sleeves (available as wire management "kits"). Reference charts, easy access to food and water, phone charging accessories, back-up peripheral devices, and the strategic placement or absence of desk phones are other features to consider. Cleaning should be scheduled regularly, especially for shared spaces. Aesthetically pleasing, clean, and thoughtfully designed environments can improve work experience and support long-term productivity.

Psychosocial environment

The social and psychological aspects of the workplace play a crucial role in influencing productivity in radiology. A positive team environment can improve work experience as well as efficiency. Optimal work culture provides a buffer against negative stresses, leads to higher quality care, and can impact organizational success.

Features of highly effective team environments include (though are not limited to):

- Interest and investment in colleagues as friends rather than only as workers. This includes seeking to understand and support both the professional and personal goals of others. Positive relationships and friends at work are known to be among the strongest predictors of work satisfaction. In-person interactions with colleagues (when possible) can help meet underappreciated social needs and foster work engagement.

- Avoiding blame and forgiving mistakes. In radiology, this may manifest as recognizing that we are all prone to error, and avoiding harsh criticism for understandable slips, misses, or other imperfections. Those engaged in teaching or leadership roles can foster a positive work environment by recognizing the varying capabilities and goals of others. Guidance conveyed without criticism can be both instructive and support a collegial work culture.

- Emphasizing the meaningfulness of work. In radiology, it can be useful to remain engaged with the impact of our work on patient outcomes and to establish collaborative relationships with clinical colleagues. Many radiologists derive professional satisfaction from providing the highest quality of care that they can. Seeking feedback on clinical work and continued professional development can meet underappreciated needs for meaningfulness.

- Treating colleagues with respect, gratitude, and trust. Expressing freeform gratitude for the contribution of others can help maintain a collaborative and positive work environment. Building trusting professional relationships allows the alignment of aims and minimizes unnecessary conflict.

Workplace culture and team dynamics are readily modifiable via individual actions as well as via institutional efforts. It is valuable to envision an ideal work culture and endeavor to cultivate such an environment wherever possible. In conclusion, the psychosocial work environment has a profound impact on operational efficiency, individual well-being, and the quality of patient care.

Selected references

- Glover AM, Whitman GJ, Shin K. Ergonomics in Radiology: Improving the Work Environment for Radiologists. Current Problems in Diagnostic Radiology. 2022 Sep 1;51(5):680-5.
- Goyal N, Jain N, Rachapalli V. Ergonomics in radiology. Clinical radiology. 2009 Feb 1;64(2):119-26.
- Larsen EP, Hailu T, Sheldon L, Ginader A, Bodo N, Dewane D, Degnan AJ, Finley J, Sze RW. Optimizing radiology reading room design: the eudaimonia radiology machine. Journal of the American College of Radiology. 2021 Jan 1;18(1):108-20.
- Laurent, J.G.C., MacNaughton, P., Jones, E., Young, A.S., Bliss, M., Flanigan, S., Vallarino, J., Chen, L.J., Cao, X. and Allen, J.G., 2021. Associations between acute exposures to PM2. 5 and carbon dioxide indoors and cognitive function in office workers: a multicountry longitudinal prospective observational study. Environmental Research Letters, 16(9), p.094047.
- Tham KW, Willem HC. Room air temperature affects occupants' physiology, perceptions and mental alertness. Building and Environment. 2010 Jan 1;45(1):40-4.
- Cameron K, Mora C, Leutscher T, Calarco M. Effects of positive practices on organizational effectiveness. The Journal of Applied Behavioral Science. 2011 Sep;47(3):266-308.
- Seppala E. Positive teams are more productive. Harvard Business Review. 2015 Mar 18.
- Agarwal M, van der Pol CB, Patlas MN, Udare A, Chung AD, Rubino J. Optimizing the radiologist work environment: Actionable tips to improve workplace satisfaction, efficiency, and minimize burnout. La radiologia medica. 2021 Oct;126:1255-7.

Hardware Optimization

Long H. Tu

E. Brooke Schrickel

Joseph Cavallo

Introduction

Improving the hardware interface can produce further gains in efficiency. Historically, programming buttons on a Dictaphones was the primary option for added efficiency. However, thanks to the proliferation of gaming and productivity-oriented hardware, there is now much more potential for customization at the radiology workstation. Specific choice of peripherals may be constrained by IT infrastructure or rules regarding what may be connected to hospital computers. Numerous individual and practice-level factors need to be considered when selecting hardware modifications and upgrades.

Links to specific hardware mentioned can be found here:

- tinyurl.com/fast-rad-gear
- (Disclosure: We do not have a financial relationship with any vendors or manufacturers. We provide examples of products for illustration, without specific endorsement.)

Dictaphone programming

Most residency programs and practice settings will use a handheld Dictaphone for reporting. Voice-recognition is already an excellent improvement over typing. If the Dictaphone cannot be replaced due to workplace-related restrictions, workflow improvements can still be made by assigning functions to extra buttons on the Dictaphone.

If using a PowerMic Dictaphone (integrated with PowerScribe), among the highest value modifications is assigning "sign report" to one of the custom buttons. Ideally, a button close to the resting place of one's thumb is used. Using the microphone to sign reports removes the need to click on the corresponding button in PowerScribe or find the keyboard shortcut (F12).

Numerous other functions related to report editing may also be assigned and can further improve the experience of report generation. Higher priority functions include the backspace, delete, delete word, and new line functions. Minimizing the need to put the PowerMic down to edit reports can improve speed.

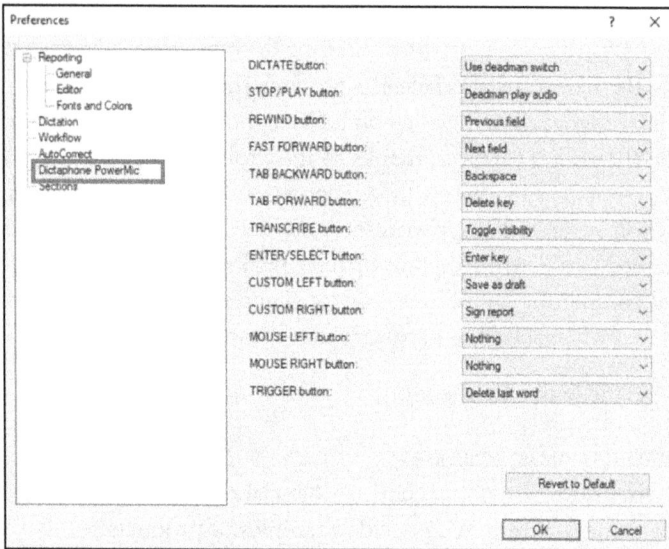

Preferences	? X

(Reporting tree: General, Editor, Fonts and Colors, Dictation, Workflow, AutoCorrect, Dictaphone PowerMic, Sections)

DICTATE button:	Use deadman switch
STOP/PLAY button:	Deadman play audio
REWIND button:	Previous field
FAST FORWARD button:	Next field
TAB BACKWARD button:	Backspace
TAB FORWARD button:	Delete key
TRANSCRIBE button:	Toggle visibility
ENTER/SELECT button:	Enter key
CUSTOM LEFT button:	Save as draft
CUSTOM RIGHT button:	Sign report
MOUSE LEFT button:	Nothing
MOUSE RIGHT button:	Nothing
TRIGGER button:	Delete last word

Revert to Default   OK   Cancel

Figure: The preference menu in PowerScribe from which the PowerMic can be programmed.

Hardware overview and priority

The greatest improvement in efficiency arises from transitioning from a hand-held Dictaphone/PowerMic to a hands-free solution, such as through using a Dictaphone holder, freestanding microphone, or headset. Next, use of a programmable mouse can provide improvements in efficiency by reducing the need to move one's hands between the mouse and keyboard for select functions. Of comparable or even greater value is the use of an offhand device, which pairs well with hands-free dictation. Scrolling ability with the offhand is a priority. Additional programmed keys can further reduce reliance on the keyboard. Specialized keyboards, a footpad, and other devices may provide other marginal improvements.

Hardware optimizations synergize with customizable hotkeys within PACS, dictation shortcuts, as well as use of automation software like AutoHotKey (discussed in a later chapter).

Hands-free dictation

There are many solutions for hands-free dictation. The ideal is perhaps a desk or arm-mounted microphone, which can be toggled between on and off states. The continuous "on" state allows dictation without the delay that occurs when using a push-to-talk function. Eliminating this pause also reduces dictation errors from incomplete voice recognition and cuts down on repetitive motion of the thumb.

If using a separate microphone, it can be helpful to position the microphone near the monitor used for report editing. However, in quiet environments, a quality (omnidirectional) microphone will provide hi-fidelity recording from any location. Placing the microphone behind monitors is feasible. Dictating may be performed while facing any screen or even at a distance from the desk. It is important to remember to toggle off these microphones when not dictating or if there is unexpected background speech.

Figure: Freestanding microphones including the Logitech Blue Yeti (far left) and RØDE NT-USB+ (center left) as well as directional microphones made by RØDE (top right) and Comica (bottom right).

Using a hands-free approach that is sensitive to sound direction can be advantageous in shared workspaces or in environments with unavoidable ambient noise. Mounting a microphone on a flexible arm allows for dynamic positioning that can minimize interference. Directional microphones, gooseneck microphones, and dictation headsets are other solutions which can be tuned to a specific range. If multiple recording devices are plugged into the same computer (e.g., a third-party microphone and the PowerMic), the device to be used with PowerScribe needs to be selected from a dropdown menu that appears with launching the program.

Purchase of a separate microphone or headset is not strictly required to achieve hands-free dictation. A desk-mounted Dictaphone holder can be used to achieve similar results. Dictaphone holders ideally have a flexible grip and adjustable neck, to optimize positioning. Radiologists and trainees at our program have found a variety of products less than $20 which work very well. The most popular is the Primens Gooseneck Phone Holder (used to hold the PowerMic rather than a phone). In some cases, it is also possible to wear the PowerMic on one's person using a shoulder or body mount, though this is not commonly done. Use of the PowerMic on a stand is feasible in shared workspaces and is the most popular solution at our program.

If choosing to use a PowerMic for dictation, it can be useful to modify the system speaker output away from the Dictaphone. By default, using the speaker on the Dictaphone precludes dictating such as while attending a virtual meeting or listening to other audio output.

Figure: A variety of phone and microphone stands which can hold the PowerMic, including (from left to right) products made by Primens, Lamicall, and InnoGear.

Commercial headsets are an alternative to both independent microphones and Dictaphone stands. The choice of specific model is likely to depend mostly on preference for size, degree of head contact, and auxiliary features.

Nuance produces an "official" headset for PowerScribe, which several of us have trialed and unfortunately found less reliable than third part products. Headsets made by Sennheiser, Sony, Philips, and Voyager are among the array of products with which we have had positive experiences. However, many in our group who have previously used headsets have since transitioned to microphone-based solutions.

Hands-free configurations with toggle-controlled dictation (e.g., activated using AutoHotKey scripts) make reporting much faster and more intuitive. We recommend whenever feasible that radiologists consider trialing this approach.

Programmable mice

A programmable mouse is often the first and most easily implemented hardware modification employed by radiologists. The improvements in efficiency arise from the ability to access functions in PACS and the dictation software without moving either hand to the keyboard. It can be useful to assign the most commonly used functions to extra buttons.

Among the highest priority functions (that I use) are to control dictation:

- Microphone toggle
- Next field
- Previous field
- Sign report

Priority PACS functions (that I use) include:

- Change slice thickness
- Toggle between MIP, MinIP, and AvIP
- Window and level settings

Depending on workflow needs, other high value functions within PACS include: draw arrow, ruler, and region of interest.

Many products also allow programming of device-level macros (multi-step computer actions, not to be confused with dictation macros.) For example, Logitech products use a program called G Hub for device programming. Control of dictation from the mouse may require use of device macros or programs like AutoHotKey. These functions can also be used to automate repetitive or complex inputs. Device-level macros can be more intuitive to create, but may have limited flexibility. The two scripts (further detailed in the AutoHotKey chapter) that I program to the mouse are:

- "Prepare Study," which, with a single button, loads a preferred template, inputs comparison dates, brings up prior reports, chooses a hanging protocol, and navigates the EHR to recent notes (and scanned ultrasound sheets if applicable).
- "Auto-Scroll," which scrolls back and forth within images stacks for hands-free viewing.

Many devices allow the creation of multiple profiles or "layers" which provide even deeper flexibility in the programming of buttons. Access to key functions from the mouse, especially paired with hands-free dictation, allows viewing images and dictation using only one hand. Automated scrolling and study preparation produces scenarios where studies can be completed nearly hands-free. These solutions improve efficiency by facilitating continued interpretative work while answering the phone, eating, hydrating, or resting tired hands. Improved access to functions can also assist radiologists with injuries or otherwise limited dexterity.

Depending on personal preference and ergonomic needs, angled mice, mice with scroll balls (rather than wheels), or a joy stick may helpful. Most programmable mice have onboard memory, allowing use at a workstation without installation of dedicated software. Mice can be programmed at home or designated work computers, prior to connection with clinical workstations.

The most popular option at our program is the Logitech G502 mouse, which is also provided as a default on workstations. A few trainees use Redragon mice (e.g., M908) or other Logitech models (MX Master 3S and G903).

Figure: A variety of programmable mice including (from left to right) the Logitech G502, Logitech G903, Redragon M913, and Redragon M908.

Offhand devices and keypads

Offhand (usually left-hand) devices can take any number of forms and are more easily used with hands-free dictation, as there is no longer need to hold a Dictaphone. Choices include programmable keypads, multi-input pads (with trackballs, knobs, etc.) or even a left-handed mouse. Perhaps the greatest functional improvement from offhand devices results from having another means to scroll through images, which is the major source of strain in most radiologic work. Use of smooth-scrolling functionality on the offhand can complement step-wise mouse wheel scrolling on the dominant (usually right) hand.

Other efficiency-related improvements are similar to that of a programmable mouse. Controlling dictation, PACS functions, and activation of scripts for automation can be assigned to any programmable buttons. In some cases, it can also be useful to program a layer of inputs that allows working entirely with the offhand. This facilitates resting the dominant hand or performing additional tasks.

Perhaps the most important consideration in selecting an offhand device is whether one's workplace allows the installation of associated software on work computers. A number of popular devices require that associated programs be installed on the workstation at which they are used. IT departments may be amenable to allowing programs associated with vetted peripherals. If this is not the case, devices with onboard memory are required.

Among the most popular offhand devices are the Razer Tartarus V2 and the Shuttle Pro V2. These both require installation of software at the workstation. Both of these devices are excellent choices where feasible, with offhand scrolling, programmable buttons, and device-level macro capability. Fewer offhand devices offer onboard memory. Keypads with onboard memory include MAX Falcon and Ecarke products. The ambidextrous Logitech G903 mouse is a potential offhand device that has the rare combination of onboard memory, scrolling capability, and programmable buttons. Use of more than one peripheral device may provide complementary improvements if no single device provides all desired functions. This may be particularly true if using only devices with onboard memory.

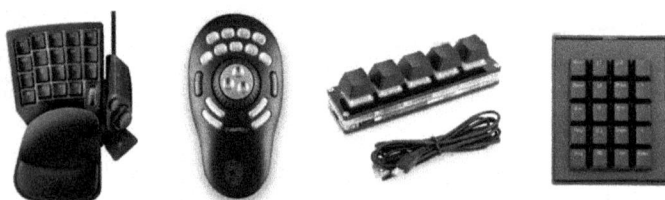

Figure: A variety of offhand devices, including (from left to right) the Razer Tartarus V2 and the Shuttle Pro V2, as well as Ecarke and Max Falcon keypads.

Other devices

A number of radiologists at our program use mechanical keyboards. Improved tactile feedback can assist those looking to maximize typing efficiency. Keyboards with a smaller footprint, through omission of the number pad, can reduce desk clutter. Number pad functions are generally redundant with other keys – if use of omitted keys is desired, access can be provided by device macros or AutoHotKey.

Specific keyboards may also offer programmable keys, knobs, and scroll wheels. A more sophisticated keyboard, especially with scrolling ability, can replace many of the functions that would usually be achieved with offhand devices.

A few companies (e.g., Philips) make devices with foot pedals for dictation. Differing pedals activate dictation or tab back and forth in PowerScribe. This is another means of achieving handsfree dictation, though is not commonly used.

My devices and rationale

My choice of hardware is largely influenced by the requirement for onboard memory. Our health system does not allow installation of third-party programs on hospital-based or hospital-provided remote computers.

In my remote office, I use two Logitech G903 programmable mice, one for each hand. They are programmed as mirror images, except the "previous field" and "next field" functions, which are consistently assigned to mouse wheel left and right respectively. The offhand mouse is usually set to smooth wheel scrolling, while the dominant mouse is set to stepwise. I also use a small programmable linear keypad (Ecarke) with five buttons. These are programmed to open programs and navigate dictation. My keyboard is a basic model (HP USB Slim Business), which perhaps because of familiarity, I prefer to more advanced options.

The redundancy between right and left mouse keys allows me to perform essentially all diagnostic work with either hand. Scrolling, in particular, can be performed with click-and-drag, wheel scrolling, or automated from either mouse. Microphone toggling, report navigation, and report signing are accessible from both mice, the keypad, and keyboard.

As I often use a desk treadmill or bike, I haven't made use of the dictation foot pedal. Use of an omnidirectional microphone (RØDE NT-USB) facilitates dictation while pacing or stepping back from the desktop.

Differing radiologists and settings are likely to have differing needs. I might have opted for the Razer Tartarus V2 or Shuttle Pro V2 for offhand use had these been compatible with our IT environment. I have changed my configuration a few times, having previously used a Logitech G502 and MAX Falcon keypad. Doubtlessly, if new needs arise, I will add or substitute devices.

Our colleagues use a variety of configurations, all of which provide similar functionality. The most important themes are handsfree dictation, offhand scrolling, and the ability to perform key functions without moving one's hands between devices.

Selected references

- Lee SN, Venugopal N, Breshears E, Shieh A, Bhargava P, Said N. Quick Guide: Programming a Gaming Mouse for PACS to Optimize Radiology Workflow. Current Problems in Diagnostic Radiology. 2023 Sep 26:S0363-0188.
- McGrath AL, Dodelzon K, Awan OA, Said N, Bhargava P. Optimizing radiologist productivity and efficiency: Work smarter, not harder. European Journal of Radiology. 2022 Oct 1;155:110131.
- Grigorian A, Fang P, Kirk T, Efendizade A, Jadidi J, Sighary M, Cohen-Addad DI. Learning from gamers: integrating alternative input devices and AutoHotkey scripts to simplify repetitive tasks and improve workflow. Radiographics. 2020 Jan;40(1):141-50.
- The Best Radiology Setup/Workstation Equipment. https://www.benwhite.com/radiology/the-best-radiology-setup-workstation-equipment/. Accessed: 11/9/2023.

AutoHotKey and Macro Scripting

Long H. Tu

Kyle Tegtmeyer

Christopher Gange

Introduction

AutoHotKey (AHK) is a powerful and flexible tool used in many fields that can further improve radiologist efficiency. AHK allows remapping of simple computer inputs to more complex actions, allowing automation of repetitive tasks. For radiologists, custom AHK scripts can be used to open programs, control dictation applications from the keyboard (or other devices), and improve navigation in PACS and the EHR. AutoHotKey can also be used to simplify repetitive educational and research tasks.

One useful feature of AutoHotKey is that once a script is written, it can be launched like a conventional program, i.e., by double-clicking on a computer icon. New users need not know how to actually write or create scripts to benefit. There are two ways to run AHK scripts: running the script itself which calls an AHK executable file or compiling the script into a standalone executable. Often the security environment of one's practice will determine which method can be used, as most IT groups block any unknown executables.

Figure: The appearance of AHK scripts as desktop icons.

Unfortunately, AHK can also be used for malicious purposes and is often blocked in organizations, specifically because it has the power to launch or control other programs. If AHK is blocked in one's organization by default, it is necessary to work with IT to come up with a solution to mitigate the risks. At our institution, we agreed to run all scripts from a single network drive, with only a limited number of radiologists having "write" access but any radiologist having "read" access. This allowed a few trusted individuals to write scripts, which can be used by anyone. IT has access to look at the scripts that are written and remove any that could cause harm.

If one's organization doesn't limit third party executables, AHK can be run from the work computer, a USB drive (to make it portable), or a practice-level shared directory. In any setting, it is good practice to have knowledgeable staff inspect downloaded scripts prior to use.

Building AHK scripts de novo is unlikely to be useful to all radiologists. However, basic understanding of functionality of the AHK tool can be of benefit to practically all radiologists. The goal of improving workflow by limiting keystrokes and mouse clicks, and having a simple alternative to proprietary microphones will interest most radiologists. This chapter will primarily discuss the use of prefabricated scripts, means to modify scripts for personal use, and only the broader outlines of more sophisticated applications.

The AutoHotKey program can be found at: https://www.autohotkey.com/. The website and associated forums offer guidance for those with deeper interest in script production. Generative AI systems including Chat-GPT and Bard are now also able to assist with script creation.

Scripts discussed in this chapter are provided in an online repository at: https://tinyurl.com/fast-rad-ahk. Most existing available scripts utilize version 1.1; we therefore elected to make all provided instructions and scripts within our repository written for AHK version 1.1. A newer version of AutoHotKey (v2.0) has become available. Future script releases may use the newer language if it can be found to offer sufficient advantages.

For those with special interest, AutoHotKey offers a truly untapped means of automating onerous or unapproachable tasks in clinical, educational, and research work. AHK scripts can move the mouse, navigate through graphical interfaces, operate with conditional logic, find specific images or text on the screen, and analyze text and other content. Scripts can integrate existing workflows with novel AI or machine learning applications. While we will cover only basics here, there remains unexplored potential to further improve the efficiency and quality of radiologist work. We encourage those interested to delve further into the myriad advanced materials on AHK (beyond the scope of this text) freely available online. In this chapter, script excepts are provided for illustration, though may be skimmed or skipped for most readers.

Design and integration considerations

Certain keyboard keys are not commonly used in dictations or when typing and preferred for assigning special functions. These include:

- [(left bracket)
-] (right bracket)
- \ (backslash)
- ` (backtick/tilde key to the left of "1")
- Caps Lock (AHK can set the native function as always "off")
- Scroll Lock (…native function set always "off")
- Num Lock (…native function set always "on" or "off")
- Numpad +
- Numpad −
- Numpad *

Uncommonly used key combinations can also be helpful to assign special functions. These include:

- Ctrl + Shift + any letter key
- Caps Lock (native function deactivated) + any letter key
- Scroll Lock (native function deactivated) + any letter key
- Num Lock (native function deactivated) + any letter key

We recommend one avoids assigning functions to more commonly used (letter) keys alone, or to Ctrl + any letter key alone, as these may interfere with existing functions in PACS or other programs. If using Num Lock, it can be useful to consider whether always on or always off is preferred, to access the number pad or alternative functions. AutoHotKey scripts can also be used by associating specific buttons on mice and other input devices with the hotkey(s) for the desired script.

In many cases, it's useful to suspend hotkeys (if interfering with other functions) or exit scripts entirely. In many of the scripts we use, "Ctrl + Alt + S" is programmed to suspend and unsuspend the script. "WinKey + X" exits the script. Scripts can also be manually suspended or closed from the Windows task bar.

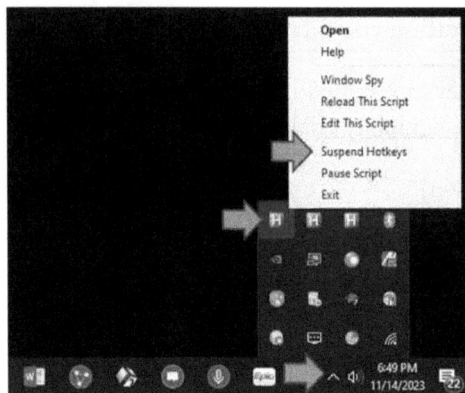

Figure: To manually suspend or close AHK scripts, click on Window taskbar "hidden icons," right click on the AHK icon, and chose "Suspend…" or "Exit" (arrows, from bottom to top).

Control dictation from the keyboard

Hands-free dictation (i.e., using a standalone microphone or placing the Dictaphone on a stand) requires a means to control PowerScribe from the keyboard or other peripheral devices. Without the PowerMic or AHK, one would need to click into Powerscibe to bring the application into focus to allow tabbing through fill-in fields (using the Tab key) or to toggle dictation (using the F4 Key). This would require interrupting attention to PACS. The following script ("Tools.ahk") allows immediate use of these commands with single keystrokes. The hotkeys are the backslash, left bracket, and right backet under the backspace key. The backtick (the ` key to the left of "1") is used to sign reports.

Function Summary:
- \ (backslash) → Turn On/Off Dictation
- [(left bracket) → Previous field
-] (right bracket) → Next field
- ` (backtick) → Sign report

Script Excerpt:

```
\::
WinActivate, Nuance PowerScribe
WinWaitActive, Nuance PowerScribe
Send, {F4}
return


[::
WinActivate, Nuance PowerScribe
WinWaitActive, Nuance PowerScribe
Send, +{Tab}
return


]::
WinActivate, Nuance PowerScribe
WinWaitActive, Nuance PowerScribe
Send, {Tab}
Return


`::
WinActivate, Nuance PowerScribe
WinWaitActive, Nuance PowerScribe
Send, {F12}
return
```

In the preceding script, the character before each double colon designates which keystroke activates the function. These could be altered to personal preference. AutoHotKey uses special characters to indicate certain keys within scripts, including for shift (+), alt (!), ctrl (^), and the Windows logo key (#). A full list of keys for AHK v1.1 is available at https://www.autohotkey.com/docs/v1/KeyList.htm for those interested.

It's important to note that the above functions do not function *exactly* like the native PowerMic buttons. The PowerMic does not require PowerScribe be the "active" window to send commands. After any of the above functions are used, PowerScribe will be made the active window (the same as if one had clicked on it); which does not happen while using the PowerMic. This slight difference however does not generally impede workflow.

In further optimized workflows, these same hotkeys are then assigned to a peripheral device, such as a programmable mouse or keypad. Report navigation and signing can therefore be done entirely without touching the keyboard (or PowerMic.)

Automated study preparation

Aside from controlling dictation, among the most powerful improvements in efficiency possible with AutoHotKey is to automate longer sequences of actions used to evaluate and report studies. In our practice, we use PowerScribe for dictation, Visage for PACS, and EPIC for electronic health records. Our current practice does not allow automatic population of personalized templates (default templates take priority). Hanging protocols in PACS (exact parameters for how a given study is displayed on the screen) can be reorganized within a taskbar, but radiologists cannot set specific hanging protocols to automatically load. Therefore, upon opening any study, most radiologists are obligated to perform the following repeated actions:

- Populate any personal template (delete the default if needed)
- If an ultrasound study, open the scanned technologist worksheet
- Navigate the EHR to relevant clinician notes
- Open prior radiology reports within PACS
- Scroll to the bottom of prior reports (e.g., to read the impression)
- Add comparison studies to the report
- Choose the preferred hanging protocol within PACS

With AHK, we have been able to automate all of the above actions to occur with a single keystroke. Without automation, these processes would take 10-12 actions, including a voice command, visual search to identify buttons, and mouse movement across multiple screens. For the fastest human users, this process takes 5-10 seconds; average users require 15-30 seconds. With automation, the process can be completed with a single action in 1-2 seconds, without visual attention or (user directed) mouse movement. On a busy shift, dictating >100 cases, automation saves >1,000 actions and >15 minutes. Over longer timeframes, cumulative tens of thousands of superfluous actions and many hours of clicking can be avoided.

The reduction in mental fatigue from reduced clicking, speaking, and mouse movement required for these actions cannot be overstated. Each input that physicians (including radiologists) are required to perform at a computer takes a subtle toll on mental energy and physical health (e.g., through repetitive use injuries). The accumulated burden can contribute to frustration and burnout. Scripts that automate a multitude of actions can have a profound impact on work experience and facilitate the achievement of a state of "flow."

This script is provided under the name "Autoload.ahk" in the repository as example. However, direct transfer to differing practice settings is unlikely to be successful without modification. The scripted inputs activate commands specific to our software, though similar features likely exist within other implementations. Full utility also requires appropriate configuration of PowerScribe and PACS shortcuts. In any implementation, steps in the sequence can be removed (deleted from the script) if not relevant or desired. Additional logic or steps could broaden functionality.

To show how such a solution could be built for any system, we sketch the major components of the script and discuss how AHK interacts with niche functions in PowerScribe and our PACS to perform specific actions. Explanatory comments are provided within the script (anything on a line written after the semicolons) to provide a guide the purpose of preceding code. Any text after the semicolons in scripts are ignored by AHK and not executed.

- First, a hotkey is assigned (in this case Caps Lock). If using Caps Lock or a similar toggle key, the default function set as always off. Separately, this same hotkey is associated with a button on external input device(s), so that either the keyboard or the mouse can be used to launch the script.

Script Excerpt:

```
SetCapsLockState, alwaysoff          ; default Caps Lock set to off
Capslock::                           ; Caps Lock key starts script
```

- Next, PowerScribe is activated, and a macro shortcut is used to populate the exam title (which works even if the exam is not yet complete). In this case, "s0" is a shortcut to a macro containing only the PowerScribe merge field for the name of the imaging exam. Implementations that use a different shortcut for loading study name can be produced with adjustment of the *send* commands below.

Script Excerpt:

```
WinActivate PowerScribe      ; activate PowerScribe
send, {click, 900 185}       ; click into textbox
sleep, 25
send, ^{Home}                ; go to beginning of text
sleep, 25
send, +{End}                 ; select first line
sleep, 50
send, s                      ; type "s0" to populate exam title
sleep, 50
send, 0
sleep, 50
send, {Enter}
sleep, 50
```

- The exam name is selected, then copied to the clipboard, which allows it to be "read" by AHK.

Script Excerpt:

```
send, ^+{Home}               ; select exam title
```

```
sleep, 100
send, ^c                              ; copy exam title
sleep, 150
```

- Any existing or default text is selected and deleted. Conditional logic is used to type the macro shortcut of a *personal* template corresponding to the exam tile seen on the clipboard. Only the portion of script related to one personal template is shown below. In this case, "xrc" is typed, corresponding to a personal template for a chest radiograph. Similar conditional logic statements would need to be constructed for all major templates one may want to automatically load. One can adjust the first two lines of this script to screen the exam type and determine the study template of interest, then adjust the *send* commands to the associated shortcut name at the line with the '; type "xrc"' comment. Additional iterations of the *send – sleep* motif can be added or subtracted to accommodate different lengths of shortcut names.

<u>Script Excerpt:</u>

```
if clipboard contains XR,others       ; check if title indicates radiograph
if clipboard contains CHEST,others    ; check if chest anatomy
{
WinActivate PowerScribe               ; activate PowerScribe
send, {click, 900 185}                ; click into textbox
sleep, 50
send, ^a                              ; select all text
sleep, 50
end, {Delete}                         ; delete all text
send, x                               ; type "xrc"
sleep, 50
send, r
sleep, 50
send, c
sleep, 75
send, {Enter}
}
```

- If the exam title (still on the clipboard) indicates an ultrasound exam, the electronic medical record is activated, and specific areas are clicked in succession to bring up the scanned worksheet. The specific areas to click (the pixel relative to the top left of the active window) to find scanned sheets is likely specific to our health system.

Script Excerpt:
```
if clipboard contains US ,others      ; check if exam is ultrasound
{
WinActivate Hyperspace      ; activate EPIC
send, {click, 520 220}      ; click into EPIC tab
sleep, 800
send, {click, 275 275}      ; click into scanned worksheet
sleep, 800
}
```

- Next, a mouse click navigates to the "notes" panel and a keyboard shortcut is used to bring up the most recent note.

Script Excerpt:
```
WinActivate Hyperspace      ; activate EPIC
send, {click, 420 120}      ; click into recent notes
sleep, 800
send !p      ; preview first note
```

- Next, PACS is activated, and the area of the active window typically containing the immediate prior study is clicked on. The PACS (Visage) hotkey to open the dictation report from the most recent prior study ("v" by default in our system) is pressed. Multiple presses of the Page Down key are used to reach the bottom of the report.

<u>Script Excerpt:</u>

WinActivate Visage	*; activate PACS*
send, {click, 2000 1500}	*; click comparison*
Send, v	*; open report via hotkey "v"*
sleep, 25	
WinActivate Diagnostic Reports	
send, {click, 150 150}	
Send, {PgDn 5}	

- A PACS hotkey to populate comparison dates to the report ("c") is pressed. This hotkey makes use of a custom merge field in PowerScribe that extracts information from PACS. The key used will depend on the exact PACS implementation. Lastly, the preferred hanging protocol is clicked (for example, 'Compare MPR' for CT studies), and the mouse position is returned to the center of the main viewing screen. The script ends.

<u>Script Excerpt:</u>

Send, c	*; add comparison dates via hotkey "c"*
WinActivate Visage	
send, {click, 57 128}	*; click preferred hanging protocol*
send, {click, 620 960}	*; center mouse on screen*
}	

Computer processing speed and internet connection may differ between worksites, impacting program response times. Building multi-step AHK scripts like this example requires tinkering with the delays between actions (denoted as *sleep* # in our scripts – which tells the computer to do nothing for that # of milliseconds) or incorporation of steps to check that required programs are ready to respond.

To design a similar script in other practice settings, shortcut names need to be added to personal templates, including one to call the exam titles. PACS hotkeys need to be configured so that the script activates functions to open prior reports and if feasible, extract dates of comparison studies. This can be accomplished via changing the keystroke for each command within PACS, or by changing the script to the keystroke native to one's PACS. Differing approaches may take advantage of the ability to populate macros through clicking into the AutoText window in PowerScribe.

What we created for convenience is a relatively simple approach which could be extended as far as would beneficial. Merge fields populating patient demographics, provided indication, and other site-specific data elements could be used to produce scripts with deeper processing of clinical information. Navigation into multiple areas of the EHR, extraction of data from notes, and interaction with additional applications could also be integrated if useful.

Study "preparation" and handsfree dictations account for the vast majority of the improvement in workflow efficiency we have achieved using AHK. However, differing practice settings may have differing needs and pain points that automation can help to address. Generally, it can be useful to consider what series of user inputs are commonly repeated in one's workflow and seek to automate these as much as possible.

Autoscrolling

Differing PACS software may have integrated automatic scrolling functions. In our PACS, it is possible to "play" an image stack like a movie. The associated hotkey is customizable and the function pairs well with use of the "all images" stack for hands-free viewing on an entire study.

Not all PACS provide this ability however, and the native function in our system does not have a means to reverse scroll. To provide greater portability and flexibility, we created AHK script that toggles between forward scrolling, backward scrolling, and turns off with a hold (at least 0.5 seconds) of the Scroll Lock key.

The script functions via automating mouse wheel scrolling, so it is compatible with any PACS in which mouse wheel movement navigates through an image stack. With this function, scrolling occurs on any panel to which the mouse is moved. The script is named "autoscroll.ahk" in the repository and reproduced below for those interested in the coding approach.

<u>Script Excerpt:</u>

#Persistent ; script is always running, unless exited
ScrollingDirection := "Down"
Scrolling := false
ScrollLockPressCount := 0

~ScrollLock:: ; Toggle scrolling direction with the Scroll Lock key

KeyWait, ScrollLock, T.5

If ErrorLevel
{
KeyWait, ScrollLock
ScrollLockPressCount := 0
SetTimer, ScrollDown, Off
SetTimer, ScrollUp, Off
return
}

Else
ScrollLockPressCount++

If ScrollLockPressCount = 1
{
ScrollingDirection := "Down"
SetTimer, ScrollDown, 50
SetTimer, ScrollUp, Off
return
}

else if ScrollLockPressCount = 2
{
ScrollingDirection := "Up"
SetTimer, ScrollUp, 50
SetTimer, ScrollDown, Off
return
}

else

```
{
ScrollLockPressCount := 1
ScrollingDirection := "Down"
SetTimer, ScrollDown, 50
SetTimer, ScrollUp, Off
return
}

ScrollDown:
Send {WheelDown}
Sleep 75
return

ScrollUp:
Send {WheelUp}
Sleep 75
Return
```

Briefly, with every press of the Scroll Lock key, the script detects whether the key was held for more or less than 0.5 seconds. If less, the script increments an internal counter for the number of Scroll Lock presses. Based on the state of the counter, the script sends repeated up or down mouse wheel scrolls at a speed typical for cross-sectional image viewing. If the Scroll Lock key was held for more than 0.5 seconds, scrolling is instead halted. As with all scripts, a programmable mouse button can be assigned to send the Scroll Lock key, allowing activation without touching the keyboard.

Automated EHR look up

AutoHotKey scripts can also be used to make intermittent tasks easier. Functions can be used to quickly open patient charts, navigate protocoling screens, and retrieve referring provider contact information. The specifics of any script will depend on where in one's EHR clicks are required to input key information (including individual button layout configurations). Below are examples of these functions built into a script named "lookup.ahk" in the repository.

- "Ctrl + Shift + O" → Open a patient chart (in EPIC) from highlighted patient medical record number (MRN).

  <u>Script Excerpt:</u>
  ```
  ^+o::          ;ctrl shift o
  send, ^c
  sleep 50
  WinActivate, Hyperspace
  MouseClick left, 30, 30
  MouseClick left, 30, 40
  sleep 50
  send, ^v
  send, {enter}
  sleep 50
  send, {enter}
  return
  ```

- "Ctrl + Shift + P" → Open a protocol (in EPIC) from highlighted patient medical record number (MRN).

  <u>Script Excerpt:</u>
  ```
  ^+p::          ;ctrl shift p
  send, ^c
  sleep 50
  WinActivate, Hyperspace
  MouseClick left, 253, 43
  ```

```
sleep 50
send, {tab} {tab}
send, ^v
send, {enter}
return
```

- "Ctrl + Shift + R" → Open a protocol (in EPIC) from highlighted study accession number.

  Script Excerpt:
  ```
  ^+r::                ;ctrl shift r
  send, ^c
  sleep 50
  WinActivate, Hyperspace
  MouseClick left, 253, 43
  sleep 50
  send, ^v
  send, {enter}
  return
  ```

- "Ctrl + Shift + C" → Search selected text on www.google.com; this will open the Windows default browser to search.

  Script Excerpt:
  ```
  ^+c::              ;ctrl shift c
  send, ^c
  sleep 50
  run, http://www.google.com/search?q=%clipboard%
  return
  ```

Template/macro transfer

PowerScribe has a means of importing and exporting macros in bulk via XML format. These functions however require administrative access; usefulness can be constrained by practice unwillingness to assist with profile download and upload. Many practices do not allow XML profile upload due to incompatibility of imaging codes and other features between health systems, as well as potential security concerns. The ability to move AutoTexts between different systems or installations of PowerScribe can be immensely helpful in a range of use cases, including but not limited to radiologists that work at multiple sites, graduating residents/fellows wishing to take their AutoTexts to their next job, or radiologists seeking to use a suite of templates downloaded from colleagues or internet repositories.

We have noted that radiologists may instead save individual macros as rich text format (RTF) files. The RTF method requires a series of actions to save a single macro and lacks a native bulk transfer ability. However, AutoHotKey can be used to expediate this process. The series of steps for import or export of a single macro can be condensed to a single key. Whole profiles can also be exported with a single action using a script that loops the inputs required for export while moving through the list of macros in a profile. The resultant collection of RTF files can be transferred in bulk via email, USB drive, or shared drives.

Our script has three functions:

- [(left bracket) → "Point and shoot" import.
-] (right bracket) → "Point and shoot" export.
- \ (backslash) → Export whole profile.

The script should not be run concurrently with other scripts using the same hotkeys, such as the preceding dictation tools. Specific coding is omitted here for brevity, though the script is available for inspection, use, or modification under the name "Save_Macros.ahk" in the repository.

The point and shoot import function can be used from the "open file" window in the AutoText Editor (accessible via File → Open File). The mouse cursor is placed over the macro to import to one's profile. A press of the left bracket key performs all the actions required to import the macro to one's PowerScribe profile and automatically returns to the "open file" screen.

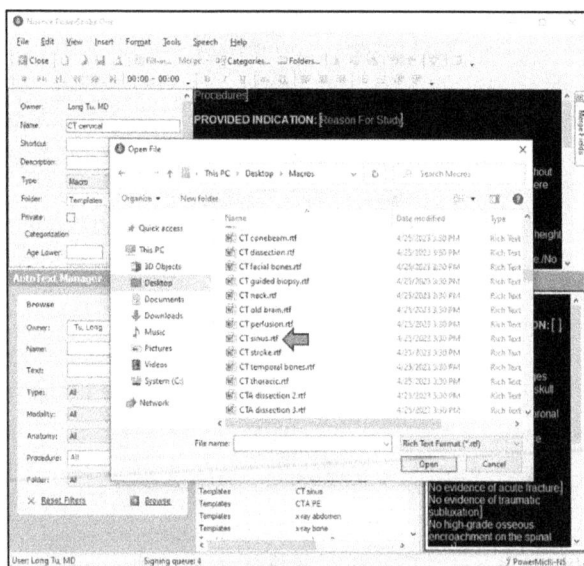

Figure: Pressing the left bracket with the mouse cursor over a macro in the "Open File" window (arrow) saves it to one's PowerScribe profile.

The point and shoot export function works from the AutoText Editor screen in PowerScribe. One macro should be saved manually prior to using this script, so that the desired save destination can be selected; subsequently exported AutoTexts will be saved by default to the same folder. The mouse cursor is placed on the next macro to export within the AutoText Manager panel. A press of the right bracket key performs all the actions required to export the macro in quick succession. Each press of the key exports one macro.

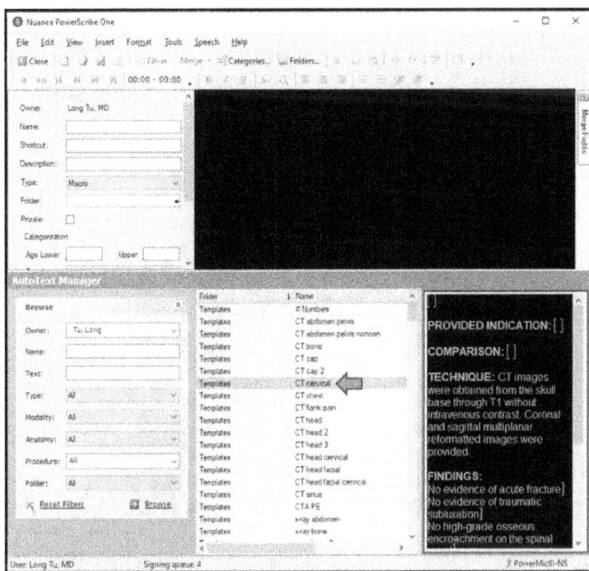

Figure: Pressing the right bracket with the mouse cursor over a macro in this window (arrow) exports it to the preselected computer directory.

The whole profile export function performs a series of actions similar to the "point and shoot" export function, but instead of stopping after one macro, moves to the next, and continues looping until all macros in a profile are saved. Of note, macro names with any characters disallowed in file names (e.g., <, >, ", /, \, |, ?, *) pause the script and could be renamed preemptively. Loop initialization requires that the mouse be positioned on the last visible macro on the AutoText Manager screen. If seeking to save every single macro in a profile, the preceding macros can be saved manually or with the "point and shoot" function. Alternatively, the AutoText Manager window can be resized to show only the first macro. With the mouse on the lowest visible macro, a press of the backslash key launches the script. If any file save issues are encountered, the script halts for manual correction, and can be restarted mid-profile. The script stops automatically at the end of the profile.

Figure: QR code to video example of this script, also available at: https://vimeo.com/872196202?share=copy ("Point and shoot" export is shown first, then whole profile export, then "point and shoot" import.)

Individual macros can be imported/exported in 1-2 seconds. 100 macros may require ~2.5 minutes with the looping function. These functions represent only an ad-hoc solution to the issue of macro transfer. Future iterations of dictation software may provide greater portability and interoperability. In any case, AHK provides a means to work around inherent IT and software limitations.

Other functions

AHK is sufficiently flexible to handle a variety of other functions. Some use cases may be too specific to the needs of individual radiologists or practices for there to be value in discussing the details of scripts here. However, it can be useful to note these areas of potential application:

- Automated communication with sonographers for QA of studies using pre-determined phrases.
- Automated communication with CT/MRI technologists regarding protocolling using pre-determined phrases.
- Automated text replacement/expansion (like macro shortcuts) and text editing for other professional communication.
- Password and login management (though this is often not allowed or advisable in healthcare settings for security reasons).
- Dictation, PACS, and EHR integration, where not already available.
- Automated look-up of text on Radiopaedia.com, StatDx, or Pubmed.
- Automated saving of case information for teaching and research files.

Whether using AHK or other automation tools, it seems that reducing the burden of repeated user inputs can make radiology workflows far more intuitive and efficient.

Selected references

- Grigorian A, Fang P, Kirk T, Efendizade A, Jadidi J, Sighary M, Cohen-Addad DI. Learning from gamers: integrating alternative input devices and AutoHotkey scripts to simplify repetitive tasks and improve workflow. Radiographics. 2020 Jan;40(1):141-50.
- Lamar DL, Richardson ML, Carlson B. Automation of educational tasks for academic radiology. Academic Radiology. 2016 Jul 1;23(7):919-32.
- AutoHotkey for Radiology. https://www.benwhite.com/radiology/autohotkey-for-radiology/. Accessed: 11/1/2023.

Automation, Informatics, and Other Efficiencies

Long H. Tu

Nadia Solomon

Melissa Davis

Introduction

Numerous non-interpretive tasks support the clinical work of radiology. Exam protocoling, professional communication, and management of business operations are tasks which impact almost all radiologists. Optimizing workflows for these responsibilities often requires systems-level approaches. We provide an overview of key strategies for improving associated practice efficiency, including automation, AI, and informatics-based solutions.

Automated protocolling

Protocoling exams is a means of optimizing the imaging technique for specific indications, patients, and clinical scenarios. In many cases, however, protocolling responsibilities can be tedious and inefficient, and can hamper overall clinical productivity.

Much of the decision making around protocol choice may be straightforward, or otherwise not strictly require the input of a radiologist. For example, studies which are always or almost always assigned the same protocol should be passed through to technologists without requiring radiologist review. Exam types with a small number of protocol options, each of which are associated with a clearly defined clinical scenario, can be split into separate exam codes in an order entry system. Each code can then be associated with an automated protocol. Such a strategy works well when exams are ordered by specialist clinicians who are knowledgeable about the specific imaging approach they would want to employ. Clinicians who do not have a specific exam type or protocol in mind could order an undifferentiated exam code which then prompts the radiologist to select a protocol.

In a quality improvement effort at our institution, CT exam codes for which manual protocoling rarely added value were allowed to automatically "pass through" to technologists. Such exams were removed entirely from radiologist protocoling worklists. Language was automatically inserted into the protocol instructions to "perform as ordered per policy." Technologists were encouraged to review the orders and alert radiologists of any unexpected or discrepant indications prior to scanning. This simple measure was able to decrease the number of manual protocols by 25% in the course of only a few months.

Automated protocolling can also be implemented using simple rule-based models. Even with manual protocoling, most decisions are made using a minimal set of data drawn from the indication, patient age, allergies, and renal function tests. Recent research has also demonstrated the feasibility of using natural language processing and other machine learning approaches for exam protocolling. Such strategies may require querying of more data elements from the EHR. While not yet widely validated or implemented, early evidence suggests that machine learning based techniques can reduce the burden of manual protocols by as much as 70%. Implementation of rule and machine learning based auto-protocolling solutions may require installation of add-ons to the EHR. Such efforts may ultimately be worthwhile in practices with high volume and complex protocolling needs.

No matter the degree of automation implemented for protocolling, it may be useful to have written reference materials detailing practice standards for technologists, trainees, radiology assistants, and new attending staff. Until automated solutions can be implemented, the aid of radiology assistants and other support staff can decrease the demand on radiologist time.

Software interoperability and integration

Most modern radiology practices will have integration of worklist, reporting, PACS, and EHR software, so that with the launch of a single case, patient information becomes available across all software modules. Integration of specific components may not function properly with remote work (e.g., due to VPN or software limitations) or because of site-specific IT constraints. Multi-site institutions may use a variety of PACS and EHR software with variable interoperability. In some cases, departmental IT can help fashion a bespoke application to bridge gaps. When systems-level solutions are not available, individual radiologists may leverage software such as AutoHotKey to produce workarounds.

Single sign-in functionality can remove the need to login both at the workstation and for each software component. The reporting software, internet browsers, messaging systems, AI applications, and other programs can be configured to load with computer log-in. Badge-activated authentication and integrated login can decrease wait time for service lines (such as procedure teams) which may have to log into workstations numerous times during a shift.

Automated findings import and impression generation

Automated import of PACS measurements and other findings can improve work efficiency. Specific ultrasound venders provide solutions for seamless population of ultrasound measurements to the radiology report. Vendor-neutral modules (e.g., Modlink) can accept standardized data from an ultrasound device and transmit values to specified fields in the dictation software. Similar functionality in PACS can facilitate automated import of measurements, image numbers, and other data directly to the report. All such solutions are likely to be worthwhile investments to the extent that they improve the throughput and efficiency of radiologists.

A variety of machine-learning based products are also available to automate the generation of impressions from radiology report findings. Related services may assist with quality assurance, and minimize reporting errors from laterality, gender, and patient-identifier discrepancies. AI based applications may assist with imaging follow-up recommendations. A variety of products are available from Nuance (integrated with PowerScibe), Rad AI, and other companies. These approaches may further reduce the need for free dictation or manual referencing of resources to guide care.

Critical results communication

Critical results communication is crucial to ensure appropriate clinical management. However, calling clinicians for every unexpected or acute finding can be unnecessarily interruptive. Numerous solutions for improving nonroutine communication have been described in the literature, including automated asynchronous delivery in the form of e-mail, text-page, or EHR-based message. In most cases, such communications require a means of confirming and documenting receipt. High acuity, high-risk, or complex findings may still require direct (phone or in-person) discussion with clinical staff. Ideally, as much of the critical results communication that does not require involvement of a radiologist is automated or delegated.

At our institution, critical results are graded by level of acuity (which can be selected from a custom field in templates). Reports with actionable though lower acuity findings prompt an automated message to referring clinicians via the EHR. Clinicians may then confirm receipt of message through the EHR. Moderate and high acuity abnormalities are directed to radiology support staff who contact referring clinicians by phone and confirm message receipt. Emergency and hyperacute pathology require direct communication. For findings with high suspicion for neoplasm or other aggressive process, another designation activates mechanisms for notification of both clinicians and patients (who receive a generic letter advising follow-up, without specific result details). The implementation of a "radiology communication center" to handle this coordination can be financially beneficial to a practice, even considering the cost of hiring staff, as patients are less often lost to follow up.

Dashboards

Realtime tracking of service line, shift, and radiologist-level clinical data provides a means for practices to rapidly adapt staffing and workflows to new demands. Dashboards can give individual radiologists feedback on clinical productivity, turnaround times, and adherence to other practice benchmarks. Studies have shown that dashboard implementation can identify unexpected weaknesses, ultimately driving quality improvement efforts which can advance practice quality and efficiency. Directed efforts, informed by dashboards, have been used to improve report turnaround times, patient waiting times, and exam appropriateness. Practice administrators can also use real-time data to assess the need for shift redesign, staff recruitment, and other optimizations.

Resource repository

Creating resource repositories for radiology practices improves the navigation of health systems and promotes adherence to practice standards. Centralized repositories could contain information such as contrast-reaction policies, MRI device compatibility, radiologist schedules, contact lists, and IT help procedures. Ideally, all such information is collected at a single access point, such as a website or intranet directory. Access can be simplified by setting the repository as a bookmark or default homepage for internet browsers in a practice. Central management and updating of repositories can reduce redundant efforts and facilitate dissemination of policy changes. Resources which have applicability beyond a single practice can serve the interests of the broader professional community as well as referrers and patients.

General	Education
Yale Email	Residency Lecture schedule
Intranet	Lecture recordings
Employee Portal/Paystubs	AHA BLS/ACLS recertification
Medhub (Evaluations)	
Yale Box	**Reading Room Phone Numbers**
Shared Drive	Breast: 555-5555
AutoHotKey Library	Body CT: 555-5555
Remote Access (VPN)	Body MRI: 555-5555
Montage/mPower	GIGU: 555-5555
	US: 555-5555
Schedule Links	Chest: 555-5555
Attending Schedule (Qgenda)	Cardiac: 555-5555
Neurorad Fellow Schedule (Google Sheets)	ED: 555-5555
DR Resident Schedule (Google Sheets)	MSK: 555-5555
IR Resident Schedule (Google Sheets)	Nuc Med: 555-5555
Attending On Call Schedule (Amion)	Neuro: 555-5555
Trainee On Call Schedule (Amion)	Peds: 555-5555
Hospital On Call Schedule (Amion)	
	IT Help Numbers
Clinical Guides	EPIC Help Desk: 555-5555
Contrast Guide	Radiology IT: 555-5555
MRI Compatibility Guide	
Scanning in Pregnancy Guide	**Complete Phone List**
Contrast Reaction Guide	Complete Radiology Phone List
Critical Result Guidelines	Clinician Number Look Up
ED/Off Hours Coverage Guide	
Other Clinical Polices	

Figure: Example central resource repository (specific phone numbers removed).

Internet browser optimizations

Small improvements in internet navigation can enhance efficiency for ancillary professional tasks. Multiple tabs such as email, digital calendars, radiology reference sites, work/call schedules, and phone reference sheets can all be set to open any time an internet browser is launched. Collections of websites can alternatively be organized into bookmark folders, which can then be launched as a group, using a single action (middle mouse button or scroll wheel press). Specialized plug-ins for browsers (e.g., Google Scholar for Chrome) can facilitate querying and referencing the academic literature when faced with uncommon or complex pathology. Extensions (e.g., Video Speed Controller for Chrome) can dynamically speed up and slow down videos embedded in any website, facilitating the efficiency of video-based continuing medical education and expediting completion of training modules.

Professional communication and scheduling

Efficient strategies for handling digital communication can minimize disruptions to clinical work. Email filters and sorting rules can mitigate time lost to spam and non-actionable messages. Flagging messages by importance and urgency can be helpful for those whose responsibilities involve high-volume email communication. Dictation of both email and text messages from a mobile device can produce marked improvements in efficiency over typing. Text replacement applications (e.g., TextExpander), device-level macros, and AutoHotkey scripts can be used to facilitate written communication in scenarios where similar messages are sent often. Batching of email and other professional communication can be helpful to prevent disruption or incursion into other commitments. Voice messages, phone calls, and video-based meetings, as appropriate, can be much more efficient for more involved discussions.

Digital calendars (e.g., available through Outlook, Google, and Calendy) can minimize the mental burden of organizing tasks, meetings, and projects. These services can integrate multiple calendars, such as for clinical shifts, professional meetings/tasks, and personal commitments, into a single view that is advantageous for planning. Digital calendars can facilitate "time-blocking" with can improve task-specific productivity by minimizing task-switching that occurs with unstructured time.

Informatics teams and professionals

Practice-wide implementation of informatics tools and automation is likely to produce long-term improvements in efficiency. However, such efforts require upfront investment from both practices and individual radiologists. To keep pace with rapidly changing technology, most practices are likely to benefit from designation of specific IT and informatics-related roles for radiologists. Select individuals or teams can lead implementation of novel technologies and de-implement those that are no longer useful. Such teams would be well positioned to lead practice-level adoption of new PACS, automation software, or AI-based applications. Radiologists with deeper interest in these areas may seek out dedicated training or education. Avenues for developing expertise are increasingly available as informatics fellowships, certification pathways in informatics (available through the American Board of Imaging Informatics and the American Board of Preventive Medicine), as well as educational material from national societies.

Selected references

- Scheinfeld MH, Kaplun O, Simmons NA, Sterman J, Goldberg-Stein S. Implementing a software solution across multiple ultrasound vendors to auto-fill reports with measurement values. Current Problems in Diagnostic Radiology. 2019 May 1;48(3):216-9.

- Bauer A, Lind K, Van Noort H, Myers M, Borgstede J. Ultrasound and dual-energy x-ray absorptiometry report transcription error rates and strategies for reduction. Journal of the American College of Radiology. 2018 Dec 1;15(12):1784-90.

- Use of an "Auto-Protocol" Workflow to Decrease Provider and Technologist Protocoling Burden in Radiology. https://www.rsna.org/-/media/Files/RSNA/Practice-Tools/Quality-improvement/Quality-improvement-reports/2022/Use-of-an-Auto-Protocol-M5A-QI-5.ashx?la=en&hash=A1ECEDF1FB8EC14FEF6CA94FA8FF5B1D BDCA0B28. Accessed: 11/12/2023.

- Cellina M, Cè M, Irmici G, Ascenti V, Caloro E, Bianchi L, Pellegrino G, D'Amico N, Papa S, Carrafiello G. Artificial Intelligence in Emergency Radiology: Where Are We Going?. Diagnostics. 2022 Dec 19;12(12):3223.

- Nance Jr JW, Meenan C, Nagy PG. The future of the radiology information system. American Journal of Roentgenology. 2013 May;200(5):1064-70.

- McGrath AL, Dodelzon K, Awan OA, Said N, Bhargava P. Optimizing radiologist productivity and efficiency: Work smarter, not harder. European Journal of Radiology. 2022 Oct 1;155:110131.

The Future of
Radiologic Efficiency

Long H. Tu

Quoc-Huy Ly

Joseph Cavallo

Introduction

Cultivating highly efficient workflows can be guided by imagining what the optimal radiologic practice might look like today. Considering how radiologic practice may evolve in the near future can help us be ready to adopt new technologies which can improve the quality, value, and efficiency of care.

A sketch of optimal workflow

What might ideal workflows look like using technology and paradigms already available today? One guiding principle is that as close to 100% of radiologist time and effort as possible is dedicated to higher level diagnostic thinking, synthesis, and consultation. All other tasks are either rendered unnecessary, automated, or handled by support staff. All aspects of care happen with as little wasted effort as possible and care mechanisms are tracked, studied, and optimized for safety, efficiency, and quality.

To achieve this goal, all imaging cases are sorted and prioritized as soon as they are ordered. Workflow managers assign cases to radiologists according to acuity as well as site and referring clinician parameters. Worklists are further tailored not just by shift, but also deeper practice-level policies concerning cross-coverage, overflow, and potential direction of specific cases to individual radiologists. The process of case dispersal also minimizes inefficiencies related to lulls in case volume or irregular groupings in high-acuity cases. Pretest stratification for acute or serious pathology based on clinical criteria and AI-based image analysis helps direct efforts towards where they are most urgently needed.

All hardware and software components would be integrated via a single login, perhaps by badge or biometrics, providing immediate access and loading of all modules required for work. Reporting, PACS, the EHR, and additional components communicate seamlessly so that patient data across numerous dimensions and time scales can be rapidly accessed and documented. Another layer of software tools composed of AI modules, clinical decision support, automation tools, and report pre-processors operates in the background, making practice as intuitive and efficient as possible.

For example, study indication, focused clinical histories, comparison studies, technical details, and perhaps simple, AI-flagged abnormalities could be pre-populated to reports. Automated extraction of clinical data from the EHR and integrated QA mechanisms at the level of reports facilitate billing and compliance. Other applications might transfer specific information from prior reports, considering interval of follow-up and any differences in technique. (A negative or stable report for any case most closely resembles a similar prior report, rather than a "normal" template.) Well-designed templates, perhaps with integrated or linked media elements, allow for rapid visual navigation and documentation of findings. Whether by pick lists, contextual reporting, automated sorting into structured fields, or AI based generation, reporting is primarily focused on diagnostic decision-making and management rather than enumeration of all possible observations. Reports contain minimal to no extraneous detail and are as easy to read as possible.

Image stacks are automatically displayed according to intuitive, context-specific, and efficient hanging protocols. Automated scrolling and perhaps even context-sensitive windowing and leveling are available. Lesion measurements, textural features, and other quantitative analyses could be easily performed and automatically added to reports via PACS integration. Lesion comparison with prior studies could be as seamless as possible, using co-registration, linked-scrolling, and perhaps even image post-processing to correct for motion, tissue deformation, differences in patient position, and other technical factors.

Additional clinical information including risk stratification scores or outputs from predictive models could be immediately available to guide diagnostic reasoning and recommendations. Relevant literature is easily accessible, automatically summarized, or otherwise rapidly curated to inform clinical recommendations. Practice is informed simultaneously by all available imaging, clinical data, and state-of-the-art medical knowledge.

Work would occur in physical environments that are optimized for maximal efficiency and work satisfaction across numerous dimensions. Lighting, temperature, airflow, room layout, noise control, and numerous other details facilitate effective work. Workstations include input devices, interfaces, and ergonomic components which make the study navigation and documentation as mechanically efficient as possible. Automation also minimizes the need for repeated user inputs or wasted motion during work. At the same time, work practices facilitate appropriate breaks, physical activity, fueling, and other factors to produce a physiologic state that is optimized for both cognitive performance as well as long-term wellbeing. The inherent occupational and chronic health risks related to practicing radiology are minimized or entirely avoided.

Work culture encourages collaboration, mutual aid, and continual learning. The social, practical, and technological environment supports the highest-level care and makes work satisfying, engaging, and perhaps even fun.

As a result of improvements across numerous dimensions, radiologists may provide greater and more meaningful contributions to clinical care. Broad-based improvements in efficiency would allow radiologists to provide consultation and interpretation for more patients, faster, with greater depth – in less time and with less effort. If the average radiologist were as efficient as the most efficient radiologist today, perhaps as a field, we would be twice as productive. Advances in work efficiency would have positive effects on radiologist wellbeing, work-life balance, and compensation. Indirect effects would also include greater freedom to advance the scientific basis of our field, address emerging challenges in medicine, and enhance the training of the next generation of physicians.

The path to optimal efficiency is likely to differ for any given practice or radiologist. Considering what might be ideal in any one scenario can bring areas for improvement into sharper relief and guide efforts for further development.

The future

Imaging demand continues to grow. The need for our services increases on a per-patient and per-encounter basis. Indications widen for imaging across countless clinical scenarios; new modalities and techniques proliferate. Demand is further multiplied by unprecedented demographic shifts. The baby boomers enter retirement; life expectancies (hopefully) continue to rise. The role of imaging grows in the public consciousness with increasing emphasis on health maintenance and preventative care. Screening, risk-stratification, and diagnosis will play greater roles if we are to reform the predominantly reactive approach to health that currently dominates in the US.

The radiologist of the future will be asked to do more, faster, and for less compensation per case. Gratefully, with advances in technology and practical skills, it is possible to keep pace and even thrive in this increasingly demanding environment. This is nothing new; the productivity of radiologists today would seem incomprehensible to our counterparts from just a few decades prior.

In the future, radiologists will increasingly leverage machine learning and AI-based technologies to make image analysis faster, more accurate, and safer. Automation tools will allow us to perform work with an ease and intuitiveness not possible today. In the distant future, it seems conceivable that physicians today known as radiologists will become diagnostic specialists with wider ranging expertise – managing large suites of AI platforms, work optimization tools, and advanced imaging techniques. We will require greater fluency in informatics, data science, and machine learning to best interface with new technology. As always, we will need to keep abreast of evolving clinical care, which will be increasingly personalized and data-driven. Training programs and practices will have to adapt to meet these needs.

By rising to these challenges, however, we will be better off. Perhaps in a decade or so, we will process four times the diagnostic volume, with less total effort, for twice the pay. Such a future could be roughly compatible with historical trends in technological advancement.

The evolution of remote work capability may produce scenarios with even greater work flexibility and potential to impact broad populations.

Radiologists today can already provide care to patients across a multitude of states. Perhaps with advances in policy and the legal landscape, we will be able to more easily meet labor demands regardless of geographic constraints, smoothing out national irregularities in access to timely and quality care. Furthermore, US physicians may help bring access to care globally, including the approximately two thirds of the world population without access to diagnostic imaging. If novel technologies make us inconceivably more productive – this is the opportunity to do the most good.

As always, the nature of radiologic practice will depend on larger trends in healthcare. The dominant fee-for-service model of reimbursement is an indirect, though powerful driver of imaging volumes. A transition towards value-based and outcomes-driven care will see greater incentives to improve selection for imaging and provide more thoughtful consultation. New paradigms for efficiency would become relevant as these changes occur. In any case, by honing our practical skills and adapting to technological advances, we will be ready for whatever comes.

Concluding Remarks

Long H. Tu

Conclusion and correspondence

We have discussed many techniques for improving practice efficiency. Differing approaches however vary in the required investments of time, effort, and capital. It can be useful to reiterate that the greatest gains are quickly accessible to nearly anyone through improvements in reporting practices and study navigation. Additional skill development, software integration, and hardware modifications could be prioritized according to expected incremental impact.

We would also like to emphasize, especially for trainees and junior attendings, that early investments in efficiency can pay enormous dividends over the course of a career. Even hundreds of hours would be returned multifold in reclaimed time, effort, or compensation. Seemingly marginal improvements can compound in effect, multiplying the benefits to our professional lives and the value we offer to clinicians and patients.

Thank you for your engagement with this work. If there have been imperfections in communication, we hope that they have not obscured the underlying message. For feedback and suggestions, including for future writing and regarding our web-based resources, please consider emailing me at long.tu@yale.edu. It would be great to hear from you!

Long H. Tu

"More than ever

Hour after hour

Work is never over"

— Daft Punk (2001)